CONCENTRATION

Developing The Power

L E A P Learning Empowerment & Achieving Potential

ISBN 978-93-80154-62-6

First published in 2011 by Leadstart
A brand of One Point Six Technologies Private Limited
Unit no. 26, Ground Floor, A1, Shram Safalya,
Wadala Truck Terminal Road, Near Post Office,
Antop Hill, Mumbai -400037.
Email:info@leadstartcorp.com
www.leadstartcorp.com

Marketed & Distributed in India by Unbound Script
2/41, Ansari Road, Darayaganj, Delhi - 110002

EDITORS OF LEADSTART

The Editors of Leadstart are a team of passionate literary enthusiasts with a creative and progressive focus. Our team includes distinguished authors, researchers, contributors, in-house editors, and writing talent worldwide. Many literary projects require a diverse team rather than a single author to write or update the book.

These projects often involve cases where the original author cannot be contacted because they are unavailable or no longer with us. Our work thus spans a range of content, from original writings to thoughtfully abridged classics, updated editions, and translations.

ABOUT THE LEAP SERIES

The LEAP series of books has been conceived as a tool of empowerment for every individual to achieve their full potential.

There are certain aspirations that every person in the world shares. We all want to be happy. We all want to lead fulfilling lives. We all want to find our soulmate. We all want a job we love doing. We all want good friends who will share our joy and sorrow. We all want to believe that there is a purpose to our lives.

While the commonality of these goals spans the globe, their achievement is entirely individual. Each person possesses a unique and mixed gift of strengths and weaknesses, special talents and handicaps. To focus our individual lives on all that is positive within us, all that is possible for us to do, to be and to achieve, we need to take conscious steps towards it. The empowerment of our lives is an individual pursuit. The decisions are yours. The action is yours. To do the very best with what one has been given – that is the ultimate achievement of a life well lived.

You Are You
First, we must recognise ourselves and accept our particular basket of capabilities. Nobody is the same. Nor is it necessary to be like someone else.

Find Your Horizons
Once we are at peace with the composition of our own individuality, we can set out to enhance our capabilities in order to achieve full potential as an individual. We can utilise all the teaching around us to stretch our talents to the fullest extent to achieve worthwhile goals.

Cap The Leak
Once we recognise our potential, we can work to minimise the influence and impact of our weak points to allow the strengths to shine in everything we do.

Row Your Boat
Every day is part of the journey. Sometimes you win the day. Sometimes the day is lost. But you keep rowing towards the shore, towards your goals. In India, it is called sadhana. That special power within you drives you to achieve what you have set yourself to do.

The LEAP series teaches methods of individual empowerment.

ഇ

CONTENTS

CONCLUSION

INTRODUCTION

The Power Within You

Every person carries two sides within their nature. One urges us to advance, to build, to grow, while the other resists, pulling us back toward comfort, fear, or indifference. The side we cultivate and concentrate upon determines who we become and how we act. Both forces exist in constant tension, but the choice of which will prevail is always ours.

A single decision, a supreme effort of will, can redirect an entire life. One act of resolve can transform hesitation into progress and ordinary ability into excellence. You can be that person. The timeless saying, "Where there is a will, there is a way," remains as true today as ever before.

History is filled with examples of people who seemed unremarkable until they awakened to their own inner power. As though stirred from a long sleep, they began to use their hidden capacities, and from that moment onward, they lived with new purpose and new results. Every individual reaches such a turning point. You alone decide when that moment comes.

It is a matter of conscious choice whether you allow your higher self to take charge or let your lower impulses govern your life. None of us is compelled to do anything we do not first choose to do. You are, therefore, the director of your own existence if you will it to be so. What we repeatedly do becomes what we are. Our actions are the outcome of training, and training is the product of our will.

Habit is not destiny; it is acquisition. People often say, "He comes by it naturally, a chip off the old block," meaning he simply follows inherited patterns. Yet there is no law requiring us to repeat what others have done. The moment a person masters the simple statement "I will," that person begins to reshape life.

Someone may have drifted for years without purpose, but from this very instant, that can change. Even those of advanced age have turned their lives around through a single act of deliberate effort. Many lament, "I lost my opportunity." That may be so, but with a determined will, you can create another. Opportunity does not visit once in a lifetime; it waits for the person who is prepared to act.

Opportunity does not seek us. We must seek it. What seems like fortune to one may appear as misfortune to another. In today's competitive world, people are often placed side by side with equal chances before them. One acts immediately and succeeds; the other hesitates and loses the moment. Both saw the same chance, yet only one moved. The difference lies in concentration; the power to decide and act without delay.

One of the most beneficial practices you can develop is to become consciously positive, to look for the good in everyone and everything. There is good to be found in all situations if you choose to see it. When you focus on the positive qualities in others, you encourage them, and in doing so, you strengthen yourself. This habit attracts goodwill, and goodwill is an invaluable asset on life's journey.

What you give out returns to you. Encouragement offered to others will eventually flow back as encouragement to you. Everyone, at some point, needs uplifting words or faith from another. Make it your practice to lift people, and you will find yourself uplifted in the process.

Life provides endless chances to improve, but whether we seize them depends entirely on how earnestly we live up to our own expectations. At the beginning of each month, take time to reflect on your progress. If you have not met your goals, be honest about the reasons why, then renew your determination to do better. Self-examination, followed by action, keeps the will alive.

Every time we postpone what we know we should do, we lose more than time, we lose inner momentum. Excuses may sound reasonable, but they are poor substitutes for effort. Most things are possible when the will is steady. Difficult tasks demand more effort, yet it is precisely this struggle that strengthens us. Easy achievements use only a fraction of our potential and yield only small rewards. The harder the challenge, the richer the growth it brings.

Do not shrink from what tests you. Every demanding task, every problem that requires patience and perseverance, becomes an exercise for your inner muscles of focus and determination. To complete even part of a difficult goal often brings greater fulfilment than a dozen easy victories. It is through these trials that we discover what concentration truly means—the power to hold one's purpose firm until it bends circumstances to serve it.

ꙮ

1

WHY CONCENTRATION MATTERS

In earlier times, life moved to the rhythm of the seasons. People were more in tune with nature, patient in their efforts, and accepting of pauses. In our present world, however, the pace has multiplied. We are surrounded by constant demands for speed, efficiency, and innovation. Every direction seems to pull our attention outward, scattering our energy. To thrive in such an age, one must learn to bring the mind to stillness and concentrate.

Concentration is the deliberate act of directing your mental energy, holding your attention on a chosen subject, idea, or goal while shutting out the noise of distraction. It is the lens that gathers scattered light into a single, powerful beam. Without it, thought remains unfocused, action becomes inconsistent, and results remain uncertain.

Many people complain that they read extensively, attend courses, or absorb information, yet little of it seems to take root. This is because knowledge without concentration is like water poured over a rock. It touches the surface but leaves no impression. The real purpose of study or experience is not simply to collect information, but to awaken awareness, to remind you of your inner power, and to inspire the will to apply what you know.

You may teach a person endlessly, but only the effort they make to learn and apply will yield true understanding. The old saying holds: you can lead a horse to water, but you cannot make it drink. Concentration is that inner willingness to drink deeply, to take what you encounter and make it part of who you are.

When you concentrate, your will becomes active and decisive. You gain the ability to direct your life rather than drift through it. You begin to notice opportunities others miss because your attention is anchored, not scattered. In the modern world, success often depends not on having more chances, but on seeing and seizing the ones that appear. Quick thinking, creative action, and confidence are natural outcomes of a concentrated mind.

Make yourself a centre of focused energy, a living dynamo whose thoughts carry strength and purpose. Every great achievement begins with this ability to centralise thought. By training your mind to hold steady attention, you expand your brain power, deepen your understanding, and increase your creative energy.

Concentration is not merely a mental trick or productivity method. It is the very mechanism by which your inner potential becomes visible in the outer world. It is the silent force that turns intention into reality. Without it, even the greatest ambition or natural talent may dissipate without result. With it, an ordinary person can accomplish what once seemed impossible.

To understand why concentration matters so deeply, one must recognise that distraction is not harmless. It quietly erodes both confidence and clarity. Each time the mind jumps from one thing to another, it loses a little of its depth and strength. The person who cannot hold attention for long soon begins to live on the surface of life, reacting instead of creating, imitating instead of thinking. Concentration restores depth. It brings you back from noise to essence.

The power of focus is also the foundation of peace. A concentrated mind is calm, unshaken by trivial disturbances. It works with precision, conserving effort rather than scattering it. When you learn to direct your thoughts, you cease to be a victim of circumstance. Instead, you become a deliberate participant in your own destiny.

Concentration is also the seed of creativity. Inspiration does not come from haste; it arises when the mind is quiet enough for truth to be heard. The scientist, artist, writer, or entrepreneur who produces lasting work does not rely on scattered bursts of enthusiasm. They cultivate long hours of focused absorption where thought and purpose merge into one flow. That state of quiet intensity, the "zone" we speak of today, is simply concentration at its highest level.

To cultivate concentration is therefore to develop both discipline and freedom. Discipline, because it requires you to guide your attention consciously, and freedom, because it liberates you from the restless pull of external noise. When you learn to focus, you are no longer at the mercy of distraction, impulse, or doubt. You act with clear intent, and life begins to align around your will.

A concentrated life is a directed life. It transforms confusion into clarity, effort into progress, and intention into achievement.

ജ്ഷ

2

THOUGHT

The Director of Your Reality

You must first realise how powerful thought truly is. It is not a faint or passing current, it is a creative energy that shapes your mind, your body, and the world you inhabit. Every visible thing began as an invisible thought. The clothes you wear, the house you live in, the path you chose to walk, all were first imagined by someone. To think is to build; to think carelessly is to destroy.

History and daily life are full of evidence that thought influences not only behaviour but the body itself. A single idea can raise the pulse or steady the heart, inspire courage or induce fear. Consider two vivid examples:

A thought of terror once turned a person's hair grey overnight.

Another man, a prisoner awaiting execution, consented to a strange experiment. He was told that blood would slowly be drained from his leg and that if he survived, he would be set free. In truth, almost no blood was lost. Yet in the darkness, he heard the steady drip of water and believed it to be his life ebbing away. Before dawn, he was dead. Killed not by injury, but by belief.

Such stories are extreme, but they reveal a truth that governs every human being: what the mind accepts, the body and behaviour obey. Thought is the invisible architect of both character and circumstance.

When you begin to think consciously, to observe and direct your inner dialogue, you discover that thought is not merely a reaction to life but is the cause of it. The events you experience, the people you attract, and the mood you carry are reflections of the patterns that dominate your mind. This is not superstition; it is the quiet law of correspondence. Your outer world mirrors your inner state.

Each of us lives in a sea of thought-forms, our own and those of others. Conversations, media, emotions, and memories project mental vibrations that influence us. Unless we guard the gates of the mind, we unconsciously absorb what surrounds us: fear, criticism, doubt. The result is restlessness without cause, discouragement without reason. The remedy is deliberate concentration on right thinking.

Thoughts, like seeds, grow by repetition. The ideas you allow most often to occupy your mind sink into the subconscious, where they become beliefs. Belief becomes attitude; attitude becomes habit; habit becomes destiny. Therefore, mastery of thought is mastery of fate. You cannot rise higher than the thoughts you habitually hold.

Good thoughts are constructive; negative thoughts are destructive. Thoughts of honesty, courage, kindness, and purpose build inner power and outer harmony. Thoughts of envy, deceit, or fear corrode the character and repel the very success one seeks. The desire to do right carries with it an unseen strength; it aligns you with the creative current of the universe.

Imagine your mind as a transmitter. When your thoughts are calm, clear, and benevolent, they send out steady waves that attract minds of similar quality. You begin to meet people whose purpose reinforces yours. Opportunities arise naturally, as though drawn by magnetism. But when thoughts are chaotic, self-serving, or fearful, they scatter energy, attracting confusion and distrust. The outer world simply echoes the signal you send.

This understanding leads to one of life's most practical lessons: every moment of thinking is an act of creation. To think carelessly is to sow weeds; to think with awareness is to plant a harvest. Thought is never neutral. It either advances or delays you.

Mastery begins with awareness. When you notice worry or resentment, do not condemn yourself; simply redirect the current. Replace the thought with its positive opposite; confidence instead of fear, gratitude instead of complaint, faith instead of doubt. Each time you do this, you train the mind to obey your higher will.

As you gain command of your thoughts, you gain command of your circumstances. You radiate a quiet confidence that others feel. People trust those whose minds are collected and whose words arise from composure rather than impulse. Such inner steadiness invites goodwill and cooperation, creating a circle of strength that grows wider with time.

The mind, like a garden, must be tended daily. Neglect allows the weeds of negativity to overrun the soil of imagination. But steady care like daily observation and gentle correction keeps it fertile and alive. Concentration is the gardener's hand that removes distraction and waters the chosen seeds.

Remember, the act of concentration is what gives thought its power. Scattered thinking is like sunlight dispersed through fog. It is warm but weak. Focused thought is sunlight through a lens, capable of igniting fire. When you hold an idea in steady attention, you breathe vitality into it. The universe responds to that steady flame far more than to a thousand fleeting wishes.

Do not underestimate small beginnings. A single disciplined thought, held sincerely, can change a lifetime of habit. Every strong character begins by mastering a moment of thought. Every discovery began as a mind that refused to wander. Thought is the root from which all achievement grows.

As the sun shines on all gardens, so divine energy shines on every mind. Yet we may plant trees that block its light like doubt, envy, resentment. Remove them, and the light returns. The forces of life are always ready to assist you, if only you think and act without resistance. Truly, you reap what you sow, not only in deeds but in thoughts.

Through concentrated thinking, you attune yourself to these universal forces. You begin to live in harmony with the larger order of things, and from that harmony arises peace, clarity, and strength. A disciplined thought is not merely personal power. It is alignment with the creative intelligence that sustains the world.

ജ്ഞ

3

AWAKENING THE WILL TO FOCUS

You can concentrate, but will you?

You have the power, but whether you use it depends entirely on your will. It is one thing to have the ability to do something, and another to summon the energy and determination to act. Within every person lies far more unused strength than the portion they call upon. The tragedy is not a lack of potential but a lack of will.

There are countless ambitious people in the world, yet only a few truly successful ones. Why is this so? The difference rarely lies in talent or opportunity. It lies in the capacity to persist, to awaken and sustain the will to act when others hesitate.

Ask yourself: *What would I like to do that I am not doing?*

If you feel you could be advancing faster, what holds you back? Often, it is not circumstance but a subtle weakness of will, the inability to decide firmly and act steadily. Study yourself carefully. Learn your shortcomings, but not with condemnation. Instead, treat self-knowledge as a map. Sometimes, only a small adjustment separates stagnation from success.

Many people wait for favourable conditions, for someone to lead them, or for life to open the perfect path. But will is not born in comfort. It awakens in resistance. Each time you decide firmly, each time you hold a chosen direction despite uncertainty, you strengthen that inner muscle. The world changes only when the will changes.

There are two indispensable elements of success: energy and the will to succeed.

Energy gives motion; will gives direction. One without the other leads nowhere. You may be full of enthusiasm but unfocused, or you may have a vision but no persistence. Balance both, and nothing can resist your progress.

Most of us will not have an easy path. That is precisely why will matters. Life's difficulties are not punishments; they are strength exercises. The person who moves through hardship learns what comfort can never teach: endurance, courage, and the satisfaction of having earned one's victory.

Look at those who have faced extraordinary challenges. The people who are blind, deaf, or physically limited yet achieve greatness. Their stories remind us that human will is not confined by circumstance. The same power lies dormant in everyone, waiting for a call to awaken. When adversity strikes, it whispers: *Now is your moment to will.*

"The Lord helps those who help themselves" holds a deeper meaning than most realise. It is not about divine favour; it is about aligning yourself with the law of action. Life supports motion. We climb the road to success by using every obstacle as a step, not as an excuse.

When you meet a stumbling block, remember this: a stumbling block is a stepping stone turned on its side. Straighten it, and it becomes your path. The people who make their mark on the world are not those who say, "It can't be done," but those who move forward and prove that it can.

There is no power in hesitation. The moment you decide, invisible forces begin to align in your favour. The moment you doubt, they scatter. Your faith in your own capacity determines how far your energy travels. Think that you can, and much will be done. Believe that you cannot, and you will never even begin.

Many people refuse to start unless they can see the entire way ahead. But life does not reveal every step in advance. The road becomes clear only as you walk it. Waiting for perfect assurance is waiting forever. Begin, and clarity will follow. Often, the hardest part of any endeavour is not the work itself but the first decision to begin it.

Most people are defeated before they start. They expect difficulty, imagine failure, and feed their doubts until the effort dies unborn. Yet when they finally act, they discover the task is often easier than they feared. The mountain they dreaded was only a hill in disguise. So start with the conviction that the road will open, and if it does not, you will open it.

Every great life has been one of conscious effort. No one ever drifted into greatness. The secret is simple but severe: decide firmly, act persistently, and refuse to be turned aside. You may face rebuffs or delays, but these are not failures, they are part of the training of will. The person who endures them without losing purpose soon finds that resistance itself becomes strength.

"He who has a firm will," said Goethe, "moulds the world to himself." "People do not lack strength," added Victor Hugo, "they lack will."

It is not extraordinary talent that wins victories, but steadfast activity and great determination. Skill refines results; will creates them. There is no such thing as failure for the person who truly does their best.

To awaken your will, begin with small acts. Do what you have postponed. Complete what you start. Resist the impulse to drift. Each fulfilled decision strengthens your inner authority. Willpower, like a muscle, grows only through use. Each time you command yourself and obey, you reclaim mastery over your mind.

With sustained practice, this inner strength begins to colour everything you do. You no longer wait for inspiration; you create it. You no longer fear the unknown; you trust your ability to meet it. The person who has learned to will cannot be defeated for long, because even setbacks feed their determination.

The awakening of will marks the birth of self-leadership. Once you have it, concentration follows naturally. A scattered mind finds direction only when the will commands it. The will is the captain of thought, the unseen hand steering the ship of your mind. When it speaks with conviction, the waves obey.

ꕥ

4

PRACTICAL TECHNIQUES FOR TRAINING YOUR MIND

The question, "How can I learn to concentrate?" is not answered by theory but by steady practice. The key lies in interest and purpose. Dr Eustace Miller once said, "The stronger the motive, the greater the concentration." That single truth explains more about success and failure than most people ever realise. You can compel your mind to attend to something for a time, but unless your heart and reason are engaged, your focus will fade.

Therefore, every act of concentration begins with meaning. When the mind finds purpose, it naturally aligns itself. Before any task, pause and ask yourself: *Why does this matter to me? What value does this hold for my growth, my peace, or my progress?* That quiet question strengthens the motive and fixes the direction.

The mind, left unguided, is like light scattered through fog—diffuse and faint. But when focused through the lens of purpose, it becomes a radiant beam capable of igniting great power. Concentration, then, is not forced attention but *directed intention*—the art of letting every thought, sense, and emotion fall into harmony toward one aim.

The Practice of Visual Recall

To cultivate this art, begin with small exercises that awaken awareness. One of the simplest and most effective is the exercise of *visual recall.* Choose a picture, a flower, a leaf, or even a common object such as a pen or a cup. Study it quietly for a few minutes. Observe its colour, texture, form, shadows, and minute peculiarities. When you feel you have absorbed every detail, close your eyes and see the image in your mind. Reconstruct it piece by piece—the outline, the light, the subtle imperfections. Then open your eyes again and compare. Where your memory failed, correct it. Close your eyes once more and picture it anew. Continue until your mental image stands clear and precise.

This exercise seems simple, but it teaches several profound lessons at once: how to observe deeply, how to retain detail, and how to hold an image without distraction. It refines perception and strengthens will. Most people see vaguely and therefore remember vaguely; they only glance, never truly *look*. This practice trains you to look with your whole being.

As this ability grows, you will find your powers of observation expanding in every direction. You will notice expressions on faces, tones in voices, and details in nature that once escaped you. Life will become richer, because you will have learned to attend.

Learning from Nature's Stillness

But concentration does not belong to the intellect alone—it is also a harmony of feeling, rhythm, and quietude. For this reason, nature is one of the greatest teachers of mental stillness. Few realise that when we truly come into contact with nature, we come into contact with our own essence. To sit beneath a tree, to listen to the rustle of leaves, to watch a wave rise and fall without commentary—these are among the highest forms of mental training. In such moments, we do not force the mind to be quiet; it becomes quiet by itself.

Listen long enough to the wind or the sea, and you will sense that stillness and movement coexist. Nature is never hurried, yet nothing is left undone. In observing her, the restless modern mind learns balance. Every act of deep listening—without analysis or judgment—strengthens concentration, because it gathers your scattered senses into unity. The mind that listens to a bird's call with undivided attention is the same mind that later listens to a complex problem with clarity and intuition.

The Power of Silence

Even children, in their natural wisdom, understand this. Watch a child absorbed in solving a puzzle. When they reach a difficult point, they instinctively pause. They grow still, rest their head in their hands, and listen inwardly. In that stillness, a spark of understanding appears, and they continue joyfully. The child knows by instinct what the adult forgets: that silence is the wellspring of insight.

When faced with confusion, try this yourself. Stop for a moment. Sit quietly, close your eyes, and breathe. Let thoughts pass like clouds across the sky. Say to yourself, *Be still.* The mind, when it ceases to struggle, begins to listen. Often, the very solution you seek will rise from that inner calm. The great thinkers and creators of every age have known this secret: that inspiration follows silence as surely as dawn follows night.

Attention in Daily Actions

The training of concentration need not be confined to special exercises. Every ordinary act can become a lesson in focus if done with awareness. When you eat, notice the taste, texture, and fragrance of your food. When you walk, feel the ground beneath your feet and the rhythm of your breath. When you listen to another person, listen wholly, without preparing your reply. When you work, give yourself completely to the task at hand.

Such mindfulness may seem small, but it transforms the mind's habits. Most of our mental weakness comes from doing many things half-heartedly. We write while thinking of a meeting, listen while composing an email in our heads, and eat while checking a screen. The mind becomes split into fragments, and no fragment possesses power. True concentration is single-pointedness, the ability to do one thing completely.

Practising this in daily life is more valuable than any complicated method. Attention grows by attention. When you teach yourself to focus fully on small things, larger challenges will yield easily to your command.

Cultivating Inner Peace

At the heart of all concentration lies *peace*. Without inner peace, attention becomes strained and tiring; with peace, it becomes effortless and deep. A mind at peace is a clear lake that reflects the truth. A mind in turmoil is a storm that distorts every image.

If you tend to lose your poise easily, cultivate calmness deliberately. Read something that uplifts your spirit. Listen to music that harmonises rather than agitates. Spend time in quiet places, or simply close your eyes and take three slow breaths. When agitation rises, say silently, "Peace." Hold that thought in your mind until your pulse steadies. Repeat it as often as needed until the word itself brings the feeling. Gradually, peace becomes your natural state.

This inner quiet is not dullness. It is a dynamic equilibrium. In this calm, you will find that the mind obeys instantly. You can turn your thoughts to any subject and hold it there without effort. Peace gives concentration its foundation; without it, every attempt to focus collapses under tension.

The Rhythm of Effort and Rest

To work deeply, you must also learn the rhythm of effort and rest. The mind cannot be driven endlessly any more than the body can. True focus alternates between tension and release, like breathing in and out. Set aside defined periods for uninterrupted work. Remove distractions. Silence your phone, close unnecessary tabs, and clear your surroundings. Before beginning, tell yourself, *For this time, this alone deserves my attention.*

During that period, let no other thought intrude. When fatigue appears, stop briefly. Stand, stretch, or gaze out of a window. Then return renewed. In this rhythm, you will find that your mind begins to settle into deep work naturally. After some weeks, the state of effortless absorption—where time disappears and action flows smoothly—will come more easily. This is the true state of concentration, not the strain of holding the mind, but the joy of being fully absorbed.

Understand that progress in concentration comes gradually. At first, the mind rebels. It slips, wanders, and grows impatient. Do not scold it; guide it gently. Each time you bring your attention back, you are strengthening the mental muscle. A wandering mind that returns a hundred times has trained itself a hundred times more than a mind that drifts without noticing.

The great mistake in mental training is to attempt too much too soon. A few minutes of genuine focus each day is worth more than hours of forced attention. Begin small, remain consistent, and let the strength of your will grow naturally. Patience and persistence are the twin supports of mastery.

Above all, remember that concentration is not repression but liberation. When your thoughts obey you, when you can choose where your attention goes, you reclaim your freedom. The scattered mind is a servant to the world's noise. The concentrated mind is the master of its own destiny.

By daily practice, by quiet listening, by purposeful work and deliberate rest, the mind becomes steady. Out of that steadiness arises insight, creativity, and joy. You begin to feel the harmony between your inner self and the outer world. Thought and action become one. This is not merely a skill; it is a way of life, a way of seeing, feeling, and being fully awake.

ꙮ

5

MASTERING YOUR MENTAL ENVIRONMENT

Overcoming Distraction

The ability to concentrate is not simply about holding attention on one thing; it is about mastering the environment in which your mind lives. The mind is like a garden. It will grow whatever seeds you plant and whatever weeds you allow to take root. Without deliberate care, it becomes overrun with distractions, doubts, and useless thoughts that choke the growth of purpose. To truly concentrate, you must learn to tend this inner space and make it fertile for focus.

Every person carries habits of thought that either strengthen or weaken their ability to focus. Some complain or criticise by instinct, not realising that each act of complaint reinforces discontent. Others continually compare themselves to those around them and conclude they fall short. Still others allow thoughts of failure or self-doubt to visit so often that these ideas take permanent residence in their minds.

Each time you think of yourself as incapable, weak, or inferior, you are quietly shaping yourself into that image. Thoughts are not harmless shadows, they are builders. What you dwell upon becomes what you live. The mind cannot hold two opposing ideas with equal force for long. If you think of strength, you must stop thinking of weakness. If you think of success, you must cease rehearsing failure. The very act of entertaining a thought begins to give it power.

The first step to mastering your mental environment is to become aware of what is already living there. Watch yourself closely for a single day. Observe how many times your mind drifts toward worry, judgment, or complaint. Notice how much energy is wasted replaying the same unproductive concerns. Most people will be astonished to discover how much of their mental life is consumed by repetition and reaction. To see this clearly is the beginning of change.

When you catch yourself thinking destructively, do not argue with the thought, instead replace it. A negative idea cannot simply be suppressed; it must be displaced by another that is stronger and more constructive. If you find yourself thinking, "I cannot do this," immediately say to yourself, "I am learning to do this," or, "I will find a way." The first statement closes a door; the second opens one. Each time you choose the constructive thought, you are building new mental pathways which are quiet, invisible routes through which your energy begins to flow differently.

Understand that concentration is selective attention. Everything that passes before your eyes, every sound you hear, every word you read, leaves a faint impression upon your subconscious mind. But unless you *choose* to attend to something, it never truly registers. Your consciousness is the gatekeeper of your experience; it decides which impressions enter deeply enough to shape you.

Walk down a busy street and later try to remember what you saw. You may recall only one or two images, the things that drew your attention. The rest passed through your senses but not your awareness. This is the natural law of attention: you only retain what you consciously attend to. Therefore, if you wish to cultivate focus, you must also learn the art of *exclusion*, of saying no to what does not deserve your attention.

Distractions come in two forms: external and internal. External distractions are the noises, interruptions, and clutter of the outer world. Internal distractions are the wandering thoughts, emotions, and impulses within. Most people attempt to control the outer while leaving the inner in chaos. Yet the inner world, not the outer, is the true battlefield.

A quiet room will not bring focus if the mind itself is noisy. You may shut a door, dim the lights, and still be lost in restlessness. The solution begins inside. Before you start any task, take a few moments to settle yourself into a calm, receptive state. Close your eyes, breathe deeply, and feel the tension leaving your body. Tell yourself: *I am still. I am attentive. I am ready.* This simple act of preparation creates an inner order that even noise cannot disturb.

When tackling new or difficult work, proceed slowly and deliberately. Haste scatters energy. You may have noticed that when you try too hard to recall a forgotten name or idea, it refuses to come; but the moment you relax, it appears effortlessly. This is a key principle of mental control: forcing concentration often closes the very channels through which clear thought flows. The mind functions best when calm, steady, and self-possessed.

Resisting distraction by brute force rarely works. The harder you fight a thought, the stronger it becomes. Instead, notice it without judgment and return your attention gently to your purpose. This act of noticing and redirecting is the essence of mental discipline. Over time, the interval between distraction and return will shorten until focus becomes your natural state.

You can train this awareness in everyday life. When your attention drifts during a conversation, bring it back to the person speaking. When you catch yourself reaching for your phone without reason, pause and ask: *What am I trying to avoid right now?* When you notice irritation rising, observe it quietly instead of reacting. These small victories strengthen your command over attention far more than occasional heroic efforts of focus.

The environment you create for yourself also plays a powerful role in shaping attention. Order around you invites order within you. Clear your workspace of unnecessary objects. Keep tools and materials where they belong. Even light, air, and posture influence concentration. A well-ventilated room, natural light, and a comfortable but upright seat all contribute silently to mental steadiness. These are not trivial details; they are allies of the will.

Beyond the physical, create a mental environment that nourishes clarity. Begin and end your day with a few minutes of quiet reflection. Review your thoughts as you would review your accounts. Which were wasteful? Which were profitable? Which strengthened your character and which weakened it? This daily audit of thought brings accountability to the mind and prevents it from drifting into chaos.

Be especially careful with the habit of worry. Worry is one of the greatest thieves of concentration. It gives you the illusion of doing something while achieving nothing. Each time you worry, you drain the mind of strength that could be used for action. The antidote to worry is preparation and trust. Do what can be done, and then let the rest go. The mind that refuses to release what it cannot control becomes its own prison.

Mastering your mental environment is a lifelong practice, not a single act of discipline. Distraction will visit you every day in some form. What changes is not the absence of distraction but your relationship to it. The mature mind does not demand silence from the world; it carries silence within. When you have learned to be still amid noise, to think clearly amid confusion, and to remain composed amid uncertainty, you have truly begun to master yourself.

There is a profound calm that arises from this mastery, a poise that allows you to work, create, and live with depth. You begin to sense that focus is not merely about efficiency but about presence, and being fully alive to the moment you are in.

Each time you return your wandering attention to the present, you reclaim a fragment of yourself. In time, those fragments join to form a mind that is whole, deliberate, and serene, a mind that knows how to direct its energy toward creation rather than dissipation.

When this happens, concentration ceases to feel like an effort. It becomes a natural state of harmony, where your thoughts, emotions, and actions all move in one direction. You no longer push against the current of distraction; you flow with the quiet rhythm of intention.

This is the art of mastering your mental environment, not the conquest of thought, but the cultivation of peace within it.

ꕥ

6

OVERCOMING PROCRASTINATION

Procrastination is one of the most subtle thieves of human potential. It does not attack like a storm but rather seeps quietly into the corners of our daily lives. It disguises itself as comfort, justification, or the illusion of "a better time." It speaks in soft tones of reassurance: "I'll start tomorrow," "I just need to feel ready," "I work better under pressure." Yet behind this familiar voice lies a hidden truth: procrastination is not a lack of time but a lack of controlled intention.

Every time you delay action on something you know to be important, you divide your will. Part of you wants to move forward, but another part resists, clinging to inertia. This inner conflict drains energy more than the task itself ever could. The more often you postpone, the heavier the weight becomes, until even simple tasks feel impossible. The moment you learn to overcome this habit, life opens again with remarkable ease.

To understand procrastination, you must first see it not as laziness but as avoidance of discomfort. The human mind naturally seeks pleasure and resists pain. When faced with a demanding task, the brain often interprets it as a threat to comfort. The result is an almost automatic retreat into distraction. You find yourself scrolling endlessly through your phone, tidying your desk, making unnecessary lists, anything that lets you feel momentarily productive while avoiding what truly matters.

The cure begins not with condemnation but with awareness. The next time you find yourself delaying, pause and ask: "What am I really avoiding right now?" Often, it is not the task itself that frightens you but the feeling associated with beginning, fear of failure, uncertainty, or imperfection. Once you identify that emotion, you take away much of its power. The act of naming your resistance turns it from a fog into something you can face directly.

The most effective way to break procrastination is through deliberate, concentrated action. The instant you start working, even for a few minutes, the resistance begins to dissolve. Motion creates momentum. What seemed impossible ten minutes ago suddenly becomes manageable because energy follows attention. This is why successful people often emphasise the discipline of starting. Once the mind is in motion, it naturally seeks completion.

It helps to understand that procrastination often feeds on vagueness. When your goals are unclear, your energy scatters. You hesitate because you do not know where to begin. The antidote is precision. Define what must be done and break it down into steps so small that refusal becomes absurd. The mind rebels against uncertainty, but it cooperates with clarity. Say to yourself, "For the next fifteen minutes, I will focus only on this part," and let the simplicity of that focus lead you onward.

Concentration also protects you from the emotional drain of perfectionism. Many people delay not because they are idle but because they fear doing something imperfectly. They imagine a flawless outcome and, in doing so, paralyse themselves before they even begin. But excellence is never born from hesitation; it is sculpted in motion. Begin imperfectly, but begin. As you move forward, you refine. Progress, not perfection, is the rhythm of growth.

There is a psychological law that what we resist most is often what we most need to do. The task that fills you with dread is usually the one that holds the greatest opportunity for development. When you consistently choose to face such tasks first, you build inner strength. You prove to yourself that you are not a servant of mood or fear but a master of will. Each time you act in spite of resistance, you strengthen your capacity to act again.

One of the simplest yet most profound strategies for overcoming procrastination is to cultivate a state of readiness. This means keeping your environment, your body, and your mind aligned for action. A cluttered workspace, a fatigued body, or a distracted mind makes it harder to begin. Preparation is not busywork; it is an investment in momentum. When your environment invites focus, your energy flows naturally into action.

Discipline, in its highest form, is not harshness but consistency. It is the quiet promise you make to yourself and keep every day. When you delay a task, you teach the mind that your words carry little authority.

When you follow through, even on small things, you build self-trust. Over time, this trust becomes unshakable. The person who believes in their own follow-through can take on any challenge without fear of collapse.

If you find yourself constantly postponing your ambitions, do not despair. Every moment offers a new beginning. You do not need to fix a lifetime of delay all at once; you need only reclaim this present moment. Choose one thing, which is the most important thing, and give it your full attention. Stay with it until it moves forward by even a small measure. When you complete it, allow yourself to feel the satisfaction of having acted. That satisfaction becomes the seed of the next action, and soon momentum replaces hesitation.

You will notice that when you live this way, time seems to expand. The hours that once disappeared into avoidance become fertile with progress. Confidence replaces guilt, clarity replaces anxiety, and concentration becomes your natural state. You begin to experience what many call flow. It is a quiet immersion in purposeful effort where time, fear, and resistance dissolve. This is not a rare gift but the natural result of a focused life.

Ultimately, overcoming procrastination is not about forcing yourself to work; it is about aligning desire, intention, and attention. It is about reminding yourself that the future is not something that arrives from outside you, but something you build moment by moment with your present focus. When your thoughts, will, and actions are unified, there is no room left for delay. The work begins, and with it, the transformation of potential into reality.

7

THE ATTENTION DIET

Managing Mental Inputs

Your mind is the most sensitive instrument you possess. Everything you see, hear, read, or dwell upon leaves an impression upon it. These impressions, in turn, shape your thoughts, moods, and actions. Just as the body is sustained or weakened by what it consumes, the mind is strengthened or scattered by the quality of its inputs. To cultivate powerful concentration, you must learn to feed your mind wisely.

In the modern world, the greatest challenge to concentration is not the absence of ability but the abundance of noise. We live in an age where our attention is constantly being auctioned off, to screens, alerts, conversations, advertisements, and endless streams of novelty. Every distraction is a demand, and every demand fragments the mind a little further. The result is a generation capable of doing many things at once, yet rarely giving full attention to any one of them.

To reclaim your focus, you must first recognise that attention is a finite resource. You have only so much to give in a day, and every thought, notification, or piece of trivial information that enters your mind takes up a portion of that energy. Just as you would not feed your body endlessly with sugar and expect health, you cannot feed your mind a diet of noise and expect clarity.

The idea of an attention diet is simple: what you allow into your awareness determines the strength and direction of your focus. Every moment of attention you give to something is an act of nourishment or depletion. High-quality mental inputs, like thoughtful books, meaningful conversations, time in nature, reflective silence that strengthen your capacity to think deeply and creatively. Low-quality inputs, such as gossip, constant news updates, shallow scrolling, weaken it, scattering your attention like wind over sand.

Begin by observing what you mentally consume each day. Notice how often your attention is pulled without your consent. How many times do you reach for your phone, not because you intend to, but because habit commands you? How many conversations or social feeds fill your mind with opinions, comparisons, or noise that serve no real purpose? Awareness is the first step toward change. Once you begin to notice, you can choose what to allow in and what to let go.

Think of your attention as light. If you scatter it in a thousand directions, nothing grows. If you focus it on one purpose, it has the power to ignite transformation. Managing your attention diet is therefore not about withdrawing from the world, but about learning to be intentional with what you absorb. It is about choosing quality over quantity, depth over speed, substance over stimulation.

A healthy attention diet involves three conscious practices. The first is selectivity. Be deliberate about what you read, watch, and listen to. Seek inputs that challenge and elevate your mind rather than numb it. Spend more time with ideas that expand your understanding of the world, less with those that merely entertain. Read books that endure. Follow thinkers who inspire rather than agitate. Listen to silence as often as you listen to sound.

The second practice is limitation. Just as the body benefits from rest between meals, the mind benefits from intervals of stillness between inputs. Constant consumption leaves no room for reflection, and without reflection, information becomes clutter instead of wisdom. Create mental space by setting boundaries around your exposure. Limit the hours you spend online. Give yourself time each day without screens or external noise. Walk, breathe, or sit quietly and let your thoughts settle. Only in quietness can the deeper layers of your mind begin to speak.

The third practice is integration. It is not enough to consume good ideas; you must digest them. When you read or learn something meaningful, pause and ask how it connects to your life. Reflect on how you can apply it in action. The value of knowledge lies not in accumulation but in assimilation. Just as food must be digested to give nourishment, thoughts must be contemplated to yield wisdom.

Guarding your mental inputs also means protecting yourself from emotional contagion. The moods, opinions, and energies of those around you influence you more than you realise. Surround yourself with people who uplift your thinking, not those who drain it. Seek a company that encourages growth, curiosity, and purpose. The human mind synchronises easily with others; choose the minds you wish to resonate with.

When you begin to cleanse your attention diet, something remarkable happens. You start to notice the difference between stillness and stagnation, between rest and distraction. Your thoughts become sharper, your emotions steadier, and your inner world more spacious. Concentration becomes less of an effort and more of a natural state. You no longer have to force yourself to focus—you simply stop scattering your energy.

Many people try to improve their concentration through sheer willpower, not realising that focus begins long before you sit down to work. It begins with what you allow into your awareness every day. The mind, like a garden, cannot bear fruit if it is overrun with weeds. You must pull out the trivial to make room for the essential. This pruning of attention may at first feel uncomfortable, after all, distraction is easy and silence can seem empty, but gradually you will discover that this emptiness is not void but vitality. It is a space where clarity grows.

To live with sustained focus is not to live narrowly, but to live with purpose. It means you no longer surrender your attention to every passing impulse. You choose what to engage with, when to rest, and how to nourish your inner world. A focused mind does not see less, but one that sees more clearly.

When you learn to manage your attention diet, you begin to master one of the most powerful truths of all: you become what you continually attend to. Feed your mind with excellence, and excellence will begin to shape your life.

ഗ്രന്ഥ

8

FOCUSED PRACTICE RITUALS

Building Daily Habits of Deep Attention

Concentration is not a gift granted to a few; it is a capacity that grows stronger through regular use. Like a muscle, your ability to focus deepens with practice and weakens with neglect. Most people never realise that attention, not time, is their most valuable resource. They schedule their days down to the minute but rarely ask whether their attention—the very power that gives meaning to time—is being directed wisely. To master concentration, you must learn not only to focus intensely but to do so regularly by building habits that draw your mind back to stillness and precision each day.

We live in a world that rewards speed and constant reaction. But deep concentration is not born from urgency. It comes from rhythm, from the quiet discipline of returning again and again to one chosen point of focus, regardless of distraction. You cannot force focus any more than you can force calmness. You must create the conditions for it to arise naturally. This is where ritual becomes essential.

A ritual is more than routine. A routine is something you do automatically; a ritual is something you do deliberately. It carries a sense of intention, reverence, and order. The mind responds to repetition not because it loves monotony but because it craves structure. When your environment and habits signal to the brain that it is time to enter a state of focus, the transition becomes effortless. You no longer need to wrestle your attention into submission. It simply follows the path you have trained it to take.

Begin by designating a time and place for your focused work. The mind associates specific contexts with specific states of being. If you read, study, or work in the same spot each day, your brain learns to enter concentration more easily when you are there. Keep this space uncluttered, free of distractions, and charged with purpose. Let it be a physical reminder of your commitment to focus.

Before you begin, quiet your mind. Take a few slow breaths, stretch, or sit in stillness for a minute or two. These small acts of preparation are not trivial. They mark the transition between the noise of the outside world and the clarity of inward focus. They also help you to detach from the restlessness of multitasking and the scattered pace of daily life. When you slow your body, your mind follows.

As you start your focused work, give your full attention to a single task. It may feel uncomfortable at first, especially if you are used to dividing your attention between several things. But the mind can only think clearly when it is undivided. When you feel the pull of distraction, the urge to check a message, glance at a clock, or think about something else, simply notice the impulse without judgment and return to your work. Each return is a small act of strength. Over time, these acts build extraordinary power.

You might find it useful to work in cycles of deep engagement followed by short rest. Many people call this the rhythm of focus and renewal. For example, you may choose to work with complete immersion for forty-five minutes and then take a five or ten-minute pause. During the pause, step away from your work. Stretch, walk, or simply close your eyes and rest. This alternation between intense attention and gentle release allows your mind to recover without breaking the continuity of purpose.

If you wish to build deeper levels of concentration, start your day with a brief ritual of mindful awareness before engaging in external activity. Spend a few minutes in meditation, journaling, or quiet reading of something meaningful. These practices act as a daily alignment, reminding you that your inner state determines the quality of everything you do. In time, you will notice that the calm and focus cultivated during these early moments linger throughout the day, influencing even your most ordinary tasks.

Another powerful ritual is reflection. At the end of each day, take a few minutes to review how you used your attention. Ask yourself where your focus was strong and where it faltered. Do this not to criticise but to learn. You will quickly see patterns, the times of the day when your mind is most alert, environments that energise or distract you, activities that inspire genuine flow. This self-awareness becomes your compass for improvement.

Remember that concentration grows through consistency, not intensity. It is better to practice focused attention for short periods each day than to push yourself to extremes and burn out. The goal is to make focus your natural state, not a temporary performance. By creating daily rituals that return you to stillness and purpose, you gradually transform concentration from an effort into a way of being.

Deep attention also requires respect for your mental energy. You cannot expect your mind to perform at its best when it is fatigued or overstimulated. Prioritise rest, sleep, and time away from constant input. Give your brain space to recharge. The ability to concentrate deeply is not about working harder; it is about working consciously, with rhythm, recovery, and balance.

In time, your focused practice rituals will become an invisible framework that supports every part of your life. They will give structure to your days and strength to your mind. You will find that when you sit down to work, inspiration comes more easily. When challenges arise, you meet them calmly. When distractions tempt you, you return effortlessly to what matters. This is the quiet power of ritual, the power to turn concentration from a skill into a state of being.

ꕥ

9

ACHIEVING YOUR GOALS THROUGH FOCUSED DESIRE

An uninformed person might say, "How can you get anything by merely wanting it?" Yet history and human experience show that through deep concentration and focused desire, every meaningful change in life begins. Desire, when clearly defined and sustained by will, is not wishful thinking; it is the invisible spark that ignites creation. It draws energy from the inner self, shaping thought into purpose and purpose into action. Every invention, discovery, or great work began as a single, vivid thought that refused to fade.

Every genuine desire carries within it the seed of its own fulfilment. Whether that seed grows or dies depends on your ability to focus on it, nourish it with belief, and sustain it with persistent effort. Many people use enormous amounts of mental energy in vain imaginings, scattered wishes, or temporary enthusiasms. But the same energy, when gathered and directed toward one clear purpose, becomes a creative force of astonishing power.

There is a vast difference between wishing and willing. A wish drifts on the wind, changing direction with every passing mood. A will sets its course and moves forward regardless of the weather. Wishing for success, health, or happiness expends energy but yields no growth. Willing them into being demands concentration, and concentration demands discipline. When you decide on a goal, form a clear picture of it in your mind and fix your will upon it until it becomes real. Do not allow yourself to drift aimlessly, hoping something will turn up. Take the helm and steer. Know what you want, why you want it, and what you must give to achieve it.

People often begin an undertaking already convinced of their failure. They start half-heartedly, expecting defeat, and that expectation silently creates the very outcome they fear. The mind that doubts cannot summon its full strength. You must feel and believe that you can accomplish what you undertake. Faith in your ability is not arrogance; it is recognition of the creative power within you. Thought and belief are partners: thought directs power, and belief sustains it.

There is an old story of a man who rose from messenger boy to president of a great bank. His father gave him a small button engraved with the letter "P" and pinned it to his coat. He said, "Son, that 'P' stands for President. Keep it as a reminder of who you can become. Every day, do one thing that brings you closer to that goal." Each evening, his father would ask, "What did you do today to move forward?" That daily focus kept the dream alive, and in time, it became reality. His colleagues teased him for years about the mysterious letter on his coat, but when he finally became president, he revealed its meaning.

This story captures the essence of focused desire: a clear vision held steadily over time, coupled with daily, practical effort. The boy's belief was reinforced every day by attention and discipline. He was not driven by luck but by sustained concentration on one definite purpose.

To desire wisely is to recognise that your thoughts are builders. The images you hold in your mind are not fantasies; they are blueprints for future events. But like all builders, the mind needs clear instructions. Vague wishes lead to vague results. A definite purpose channels all your mental forces in one direction, awakening resources within you that might otherwise sleep forever. When you move with purpose, your energy becomes magnetic; it attracts people, ideas, and opportunities that correspond with your dominant thought.

This inner law is what we call the Mental Demand. It is the deep, concentrated call of the mind that draws to itself the conditions necessary for achievement. It is not superstition or magic; it is a principle as natural as gravity. When you think intently about a goal, believing in its possibility and acting consistently toward it, your mind begins to operate in harmony with the forces that make that goal attainable. You notice opportunities you would have missed, meet people who can help, or receive sudden insight at the right moment. The world responds because you have made a clear mental claim upon it.

The Mental Demand must be made with your whole being—thought, feeling, and will combined. It cannot be half-hearted or uncertain. When you so completely desire something that every contrary idea is excluded, you release an extraordinary power. You become like a lens concentrating sunlight into a single point of fire.

Such singleness of purpose is rare, but when achieved, it can move mountains.

The man who says, "I will find a way or make one," is expressing this power. It is the same force that drives the scientist to persist through failure, the artist to refine a vision through endless attempts, or the parent to sacrifice for a child's future. This inner command turns potential into performance. It is the silent voice that says, "There must be a way, and I will discover it," and then acts until the way is found.

To cultivate this mental strength, begin by recognising the difference between distraction and devotion. Most people dissipate their power by trying to satisfy many small desires at once. They spend their days chasing whims instead of fulfilling purposes. Each new interest pulls their energy away from the last, leaving nothing fully realised. The person who chooses one worthy goal and devotes themselves to it gathers strength every day. The one who chases ten desires gains only exhaustion.

The Mental Demand is not an imaginary power. It is the direct application of will and focus. When you hold a goal steadily in your mind and refuse to give energy to doubt or fear, you activate the brain centres associated with creative thought and action. You become more alert, more intuitive, and more resilient. You attract the means, knowledge, and strength you need because your mind is aligned with your purpose.

There is within you a silent force that never ceases urging you toward growth and achievement. It is this force that gives rise to inspiration, courage, and insight. When you become conscious of it, you gain access to a source of energy that cannot be exhausted. It is the source of invention, of genius, of endurance. When you ignore it, you drift; when you obey it, you rise.

No one ever truly fails who learns to rely on this inner power. It speaks through intuition and quiet conviction. It steadies you when you falter, guides you when confused, and restores courage when you are afraid. Without awareness of it, people wander from goal to goal, always beginning and rarely finishing. With awareness of it, you find clarity, purpose, and peace, even in struggle.

To develop this force, practice thinking with intensity but without tension. Sit quietly, close your eyes, and picture your goal clearly. Feel its reality; imagine the sense of completion, the relief, and the joy of success. Let this feeling fill you as if the goal were already achieved. Then open your eyes and begin to act on whatever the next step appears. This is how the inner and outer cooperate. The thought creates the model, and action builds upon it.

You may not always see progress at once. The invisible work often happens long before results appear. But persistence is the test of true desire. Perseverance is the difference between the dreamer and the achiever. The person who continues despite discouragement discovers that obstacles are not barriers but teachers, each one strengthening the will. Every time you overcome resistance, you prove to yourself that your desire is stronger than circumstance.

When this inner conviction becomes steady, the results may seem almost effortless. Things begin to fall into place. Ideas arise exactly when needed. You find yourself at the right place at the right time, not because of chance, but because your thoughts and actions are finally in harmony. This is the natural law of concentration: that which you think about with purpose and faith begins to move toward you, even as you move toward it.

Reflection Exercise To Get You Started:

Choose one meaningful goal. Write it clearly and specifically, then sit quietly for a few minutes each day and picture it as if it were already achieved. Feel gratitude for its fulfilment. Let your mind dwell not on how far away it is, but on the sense of confidence that it *is* unfolding. Then act on any impulse toward that goal, however small. This daily practice aligns your inner command with outer action, making thought and effort one continuous stream.

ꕤ

10

CONCENTRATION FOR PROFESSIONAL SUCCESS

In the fast-paced world of business and professional life, concentration is not merely an advantage. It is often the very foundation of success. In an environment where time, innovation, and judgment define progress, your ability to direct your mental energy fully toward one objective can determine the difference between mediocrity and mastery.

Every great achievement in commerce, art, or leadership begins with a mind that knows how to hold steady attention. The ability to concentrate transforms work from mechanical effort into intelligent creation. When you bring focused awareness to your professional life, you stop reacting to circumstances and begin shaping them. You develop the power to think clearly under pressure, to remain calm amid chaos, and to make decisions guided by insight rather than impulse.

When you approach your work with focused, positive thought, you radiate confidence. Others feel it even before you speak. The quiet assurance of a concentrated mind inspires trust because it reflects clarity and self-control. People are instinctively drawn to those who seem centred and decisive. In contrast, the scattered or anxious mind transmits uncertainty. Colleagues hesitate, subordinates lose direction, and clients feel uneasy without knowing why. Thought has vibration, and the vibration of a confident, concentrated person uplifts the atmosphere around them.

This is why mental discipline is one of the most valuable professional assets you can develop. It enhances communication, strengthens leadership, and builds credibility. A concentrated person listens more deeply, understands more quickly, and responds with precision. They are not easily swayed by gossip, emotional reactions, or temporary obstacles. Their presence itself creates order.

In business, where opportunities are fleeting and decisions must often be made with incomplete information, concentration becomes the anchor of sound judgment. When your attention is fragmented, small problems appear large, and simple solutions are overlooked. But when your mind is calm and focused, patterns emerge where others see confusion. You begin to anticipate outcomes, connect ideas, and see beneath the surface of situations. This depth of understanding gives you a distinct advantage, and 2allows you to act with foresight rather than haste.

Concentration also safeguards against one of the most common modern pitfalls: busyness without productivity. Many people mistake constant activity for effectiveness, yet real progress arises not from doing more, but from doing what matters most with full attention. When you learn to focus on one essential task at a time, your efficiency multiplies. The quality of your work improves, and the satisfaction of seeing meaningful results reinforces your motivation.

A professional who masters concentration gains what could be called "mental stamina." Just as an athlete trains the body to sustain performance, the mind must be trained to sustain focus. The scattered mind tires quickly because it expends energy on distractions. The concentrated mind conserves energy, channelling it toward the chosen goal. This is why people of great accomplishment often seem tireless—their energy is unified and purposeful, not divided.

To cultivate such focus in your professional life, begin with intention. Before starting a task, take a brief moment to clarify your purpose. Ask yourself, "What exactly do I want to achieve right now?" This single act of mental preparation aligns your thoughts and creates direction. Once you begin, commit fully. Set aside other tasks, silence unnecessary interruptions, and enter fully into your work. You will notice that even a single hour of such undistracted attention often produces more progress than several hours of divided effort.

Another aspect of professional concentration lies in managing relationships. In meetings, conversations, and collaborations, the ability to give your full attention to another person is rare and powerful. When you listen completely, you understand not just the words but the intent behind them. People feel valued in your presence. They open up, communicate honestly, and begin to trust you. Concentration in human interaction is one of the strongest forms of leadership, for it creates alignment through presence rather than authority.

Concentration also nurtures creativity, which is the lifeblood of modern enterprise. When you quiet the constant chatter of the mind, ideas arise naturally. Innovation is not a product of frantic effort but of relaxed, sustained attention. Many of the world's most successful thinkers and entrepreneurs schedule periods of uninterrupted focus each day, not to work harder, but to think more clearly. They understand that true insight cannot emerge in a mind perpetually reacting; it appears only when the mind is still enough to perceive it.

You cannot reach your full professional potential until you learn to consciously direct your thoughts toward your chosen objectives. Success in the outer world is always preceded by mastery of the inner one. The universe is filled with invisible forces, of thought, of will, of creative energy, and the more harmoniously you align your own inner forces, the more powerfully you can act within it. Whether your place in that vast network becomes significant depends on how well you can direct these energies through focus and purpose.

A concentrated mind does not merely adapt to the demands of modern work; it rises above them. It turns pressure into clarity, challenge into growth, and chaos into opportunity. In cultivating the discipline of focus, you also cultivate the quiet strength that others instinctively follow. The professional who commands his or her own mind ultimately commands the course of their work, their career, and their destiny.

ഗ്ഗ

11

ENHANCING MEMORY THROUGH ATTENTIVE FOCUS

Memory is not merely the power to retain; it is the art of giving full attention. Forgetfulness, more often than not, is not a sign of poor intellect or age, but of a scattered mind. When we say we have "forgotten" something, it usually means that we never truly noticed it in the first place. The key to memory, therefore, lies not in rote repetition but in the quality of attention we give at the moment an impression is formed.

A person forgets because they do not concentrate their mind on the purpose, especially at the moment it is conceived. We remember only what has been allowed to make a deep impression upon us. The mind, much like soft clay, holds only those impressions that are pressed firmly. Everything else leaves a faint trace that is soon smoothed over by the next distraction.

Imagine a common situation: a husband is handed a letter to mail. He absentmindedly slips it into his pocket, preoccupied with thoughts of his day, and forgets all about it. His memory is not faulty as his attention was never truly present when the letter entered his awareness. Had he consciously registered the task, forming a clear mental connection, "I will post this letter at the box on the next corner when I pass it" then the act of seeing the mailbox would have instantly brought the letter to mind.

The same principle applies to more complex or significant matters. Suppose you are told to visit a colleague or client during your lunch break. If you merely nod and move on, the instruction is likely to slip your mind amidst the day's demands. But if, at the moment you receive the information, you visualise yourself walking into that office during lunch, imagine the route you will take, or link it to another familiar detail, such as the corner or building name, you have anchored the idea in your mind. The association deepens the impression, ensuring recall when the moment arrives.

Memory works by connection. The more associations an idea has, the more paths your mind can take to find it again. One of the simplest ways to strengthen memory is to consciously weave new information into the web of what you already know. When you learn a name, connect it to a familiar word, image, or quality. When you read a fact, tie it to an existing idea or experience. Every connection serves as a thread that leads back to the memory later.

The mind is governed by laws of association. Ideas that enter together emerge together, each one acting as a signal that summons the others. You can use this law to your advantage. When forming a new memory, surround it with sensory or emotional context, the sight, sound, or feeling connected to it. For example, when you meet someone new, repeat their name aloud as you notice a distinctive feature about them or the place where you met. Later, that visual or situational cue will automatically call their name to mind.

The same method applies to learning and studying. Instead of mechanically reading or listening, pause to reflect on what you've just encountered. Ask yourself how it fits into what you already understand. Try to rephrase it in your own words. The very act of forming associations, whether verbal, visual, or conceptual, transforms fleeting knowledge into something the mind holds firmly.

Concentration is the bridge between perception and memory. Without focused attention, even the most important details can vanish. But with deliberate awareness, even the smallest facts become fixed within you. The person who trains their attention not only remembers better, but also begins to think more clearly, since memory and concentration are twin faculties of the same mind.

Training your memory, therefore, is not about forcing recall through strain, but about learning to pay full attention at the moment of impression. When you form the habit of concentrating on your purpose, when you truly *notice* what you are doing, then memory becomes almost effortless. It ceases to be a struggle and becomes a natural function of an orderly mind.

In practical terms, there are a few habits worth cultivating. First, slow down. Memory weakens under haste because the mind moves on before impressions have settled. Give your mind a moment to register what it encounters—a name, a task, an idea. Second, visualise. Turn abstract information into concrete imagery or mental scenes. The mind remembers pictures more easily than words. Third, repeat consciously. When something is worth remembering, recall it to mind a few times in different ways. Speak it, write it, or think of it in connection to something else. This repetition is not mechanical drilling but reinforcement through attention.

In time, these habits will transform your relationship with memory. You will find that forgetfulness diminishes not because your memory has improved, but because your mind has become more present. Each moment of awareness leaves a clearer imprint. You begin to rely on your mind as a trustworthy companion rather than a fickle one.

The person who trains the memory through attention possesses a great professional and personal advantage. In study, in conversation, in daily work, they are alert and dependable. They listen deeply, recall details accurately, and act with confidence. Their memory becomes not merely a storehouse of facts but a living tool of understanding.

Memory is one of the most powerful servants of concentration, and concentration, in turn, is the guardian of memory. When the two are harmonised, the mind becomes luminous, capable of grasping knowledge and retaining it effortlessly. Forgetfulness fades not through force but through awareness. Attention, sustained and gentle, is the art that keeps the mind alive.

ஐ

12

THE BODY SUPPORTS THE MIND

Physical Foundations of Concentration

The power to concentrate is not only a function of the mind; it depends just as much on the condition of the body that houses it. You cannot expect the mind to think clearly when the body is fatigued, tense, or neglected. The mind and body are not separate instruments working in isolation. They are two aspects of a single living system. When one suffers, the other weakens. When one is strengthened and disciplined, the other grows in harmony.

A clear and steady mind requires a foundation of physical stability. The simplest physical habits such as breathing, posture, sleep, diet, and movement, all influence how easily you can focus. Many people attempt to cultivate concentration solely through mental effort, forgetting that thought itself is a form of energy that draws upon the vitality of the body. The more balanced and rested your physical system, the steadier your mental focus will be.

Start with breathing. It is the bridge between body and mind, the most immediate tool you have for influencing your inner state. When your breathing is shallow or irregular, your thoughts become restless. When your breath is deep and calm, your mind begins to mirror that calmness. Before any act of deep work, pause and take slow, deliberate breaths. Feel the rhythm of inhaling and exhaling as you settle your awareness. With each breath, you gather your scattered energy and return to the present moment. This simple act of conscious breathing can quiet the mind more effectively than any amount of force or willpower.

Posture, too, has a direct influence on thought. The way you hold your body affects not only your comfort but also your state of alertness. When you slump or sit in positions that constrict the chest or compress the abdomen, your breathing becomes shallow and your energy drains away. When you sit upright, balanced yet relaxed, your body allows for freer breathing, better circulation, and greater alertness. The ancients knew this long before science confirmed it: an erect spine supports an erect mind. The body, poised and open, becomes an instrument through which the mind can move freely.

Rest and sleep form another cornerstone of concentration. A tired brain cannot hold attention for long. Fatigue reduces willpower, dulls perception, and weakens memory. The mind's ability to focus is not a matter of constant exertion but of proper recovery. The rhythm of effort and renewal, work followed by rest, is essential for sustained productivity. When you sleep deeply, your brain processes information, strengthens neural pathways, and restores balance to the nervous system. To neglect rest is to dull the very tool you depend upon for concentration.

Food and exercise, too, play a subtle but profound role. What you eat becomes the material for your thoughts as much as for your body. A heavy, unbalanced diet clouds the mind and makes it sluggish; a light, nourishing diet supports clarity. Regular physical activity, even in modest forms such as walking, stretching, or mindful movement, improves circulation and oxygenation, which in turn feeds the brain. When the body is active and alive, the mind feels more awake, alert, and ready to concentrate.

A simple yet powerful practice for uniting body and mind is to begin your day with a few minutes of stillness followed by gentle movement. Sit quietly for a short while, breathing evenly and observing your thoughts. Then rise and stretch, allowing your body to awaken naturally. These few moments set the tone for the entire day. They remind you that calmness and energy can coexist, and that focus does not mean tension, and relaxation does not mean passivity.

You will notice that when the body is well cared for, concentration comes more naturally. When your posture is easy, your breathing rhythmic, and your energy balanced, your thoughts flow without strain. But when the body is tense, the mind mirrors that tension. You cannot think clearly when your shoulders are tight or your head aches from exhaustion. To cultivate concentration, therefore, you must treat your body not as a burden but as an ally, the vessel through which your mental energy finds expression.

Mental poise is impossible without physical harmony. The greatest thinkers, artists, and leaders have understood this instinctively. They did not see physical discipline as separate from intellectual work but as its natural complement. A few minutes of quiet breathing, a walk in the fresh air, or the habit of maintaining composure even in small daily actions — these are not trivial matters. They form the unseen roots from which strong, enduring concentration grows.

If you ever find your mind restless or scattered, begin with the body. Straighten your posture. Breathe slowly and deeply. Allow your muscles to relax and your pulse to slow. You will find that the mind follows. The state of the body is a mirror in which the state of the mind is reflected. Balance one, and you balance the other.

Concentration, then, is not simply a mental exercise but a way of living. It begins in the mind, but it is sustained through the body. To care for your physical well-being is to care for your capacity to think, to decide, and to create. The calm mind rests on the calm body, and both together form the foundation of all achievement.

13

BUILDING INNER STRENGTH

Focus on Courage and Poise

Courage is the backbone of human character. It is the quiet strength that steadies us when fear, doubt, or difficulty stand in our way. Every great achievement, every worthwhile endeavour, every moment of real progress begins with courage, the willingness to act in the face of uncertainty. A person with courage is not one who never feels fear, but one who refuses to let fear decide their course of action.

The person of courage possesses persistence and conviction. They stand by what they believe, and they follow their belief with action. They are not reckless but resolute. This inner strength draws to them all the moral qualities and mental forces that make a human being powerful: confidence, decisiveness, determination, and self-trust. The person without courage, on the other hand, unconsciously attracts the opposites of these traits: hesitation, doubt, indecision, and weakness of purpose.

Concentration on courage is one of the most vital exercises in building personal power. When you concentrate your mind on courage, you are not merely thinking brave thoughts; you are training your inner forces to respond to life with confidence instead of fear. A person without courage sees new problems as threats rather than opportunities. Before even beginning, they list all the reasons something cannot be done, and failure becomes a self-fulfilling prophecy. But when you approach a challenge with the belief that it can be overcome, you summon the creative forces of your mind to find a way through.

The difference between those who advance and those who stagnate is often not talent or circumstance, but courage, the courage to begin, to persist, and to face uncertainty without retreating.

Lack of courage destroys confidence in oneself. It weakens resolve and replaces self-reliance with dependency. The person without courage is easily swayed by other people's opinions, blaming fate or bad luck when things go wrong, instead of recognising that their own hesitation has closed the door to opportunity. Every great success has been born from the decision to act despite fear.

Courage begins with desire. You must first have the courage to *want* something deeply. A half-hearted wish has no creative power, but a burning desire, backed by strong will and concentration, reshapes the very conditions around you. When your desire is sincere and intense, it gathers the mental and moral forces of your being to make it real. It changes the tone of your thought, the firmness of your step, the energy of your presence.

The person with courage commands life, whether on a battlefield, in business, or in personal growth. What is courage, then? It is simply the will to do. It takes no more energy to be courageous than to be cowardly; the difference lies in direction. One focuses energy forward, the other backwards. Courage is trained through choice: by deciding again and again to act where fear would have held you still.

Fear wastes energy; courage channels it. Cowardice scatters both mental and moral strength; courage gathers them. Every time you choose action over avoidance, you strengthen your will. Every time you hold your mind steady under pressure, you teach yourself poise.

Start today with the belief that there is no reason you cannot be courageous. If fearful thoughts arise, cast them aside as you would a poisonous snake. Train yourself to avoid feeding on negative thoughts about yourself or others. The mind that entertains fear makes fear real; the mind that dwells on courage builds the very strength it imagines.

When you face new challenges, remind yourself: "I am courageous." The moment doubt enters, replace it with faith in your own capacity to act. Remember that you are the master of your thoughts. What you habitually think, you become. A simple affirmation can work wonders when charged with belief and repetition:

"I have courage because I desire it, because I need it, because I use it, and because I refuse to be weakened by fear."

There is no justification for losing courage. The troubles that come from lacking it are far worse than any difficulty you could encounter with it. As the saying goes, *the only thing to fear is fear itself.*

Do not let the opinions of others define what you can do. No one outside you can truly measure your potential, because no one else knows the full reach of your inner strength. Most people see only the surface, the limitations that appear obvious. They cannot see the power that grows within a determined mind. But you can. You can discover it each time you refuse to surrender.

The history of progress is filled with examples of people who defied the judgments of their age. Countless discoveries, inventions, and works of art were once declared impossible, until someone with courage proved otherwise. If you can conceive something clearly, it is not beyond your reach. Imagination itself is proof of potential. The very fact that you can *think* it means it belongs to the realm of possibility.

Poise, like courage, is born of concentration. A person who can hold their mind steady under tension remains calm while others lose control. Mental poise is not indifference but mastery. It is the ability to keep inner balance when outer conditions are uncertain. It is the quiet confidence that comes from knowing that your reactions belong to you, not to circumstance.

The scattered mind is easily upset; the concentrated mind remains composed. Poise grows naturally from the same habits that produce courage — deliberate thought, calm breathing, and the refusal to yield to panic or doubt. When the mind is quiet, it can draw on deeper sources of wisdom and strength.

There must be inner stillness before the higher self, the deeper consciousness that guides us, can work in harmony with the active mind. When concentration is strong, peace of mind follows. And when you have peace of mind, you are not timid, anxious, or fearful. You stop being disturbed by outer events because you no longer identify yourself with them. You begin to see yourself as a spark of the infinite, a conscious manifestation of the creative principle that fills all existence.

Think of yourself as a child of the infinite, possessing boundless potential. Write on a piece of paper, "I have the power to do and to be whatever I wish to do and be." Keep this where you can see it, and repeat it until it becomes part of your inner truth. As you think, so you become. As you believe, so you act.

When courage and poise unite, they form an unshakable foundation for success. The courageous mind dares; the poised mind endures. Together, they create a character that neither fear nor failure can defeat.

ฦ๑ๆ

14

FLOW AND RECOVERY

Sustaining Peak Focus

Concentration is not merely the ability to fix your attention; it is also the art of maintaining that attention over time. Many people can focus for short bursts, but few can sustain clarity and intensity without strain. True mastery of concentration involves understanding not only how to focus deeply but also how to renew that focus through rest, rhythm, and recovery.

The human mind, like any living instrument, cannot perform at its highest pitch indefinitely. It functions best in cycles of exertion and renewal, tension and relaxation, focus and reflection. To concentrate without balance is to invite exhaustion; to rest without purpose is to drift into stagnation. The secret lies in learning to alternate between the two consciously and harmoniously.

There is a state in which effort disappears and action flows easily, a state often called *flow*. In this state, the mind and body work as one, attention is fully absorbed in the task, and distractions fade into silence. Time seems to stretch or vanish; you act without hesitation because thought and doing have merged into one motion. Every artist, athlete, inventor, or creator who has tasted this experience knows its rare power. It is the natural reward of deep concentration.

Flow cannot be forced. It arises when several conditions come together, suuch as clear goals, complete presence, a challenge that matches your skill, and freedom from distraction. You enter flow when your attention ceases to oscillate between past and future, when self-consciousness fades, and only the work remains. It is the moment when concentration transforms from effort into effortless precision.

To experience this state more often, cultivate the habit of preparing the mind. Before beginning your work, take a few quiet moments to settle your thoughts. Clarify your purpose: what, exactly, do you wish to accomplish? Then remove all unnecessary interruptions and commit yourself fully to the present moment. Begin calmly, without rushing. The steadiness of your beginning determines the quality of your flow.

But flow alone is not enough. Just as vital is recovery, the deliberate renewal of your energy after periods of deep mental exertion. Many mistake fatigue for failure of will, when it is simply the body and mind asking for restoration. Concentration requires energy, and energy must be replenished. Without conscious recovery, your focus gradually dulls, your creativity wanes, and even simple tasks begin to feel heavy.

Recovery is not idleness; it is part of the same rhythm as focus. It is the moment when the mind integrates what it has learned, restores balance, and prepares for the next ascent. The most successful individuals, in business, science, or art, are not those who work endlessly, but those who understand how to balance their intensity with renewal.

There are many ways to recover the mind and spirit. Quiet reflection is one of the simplest. After a period of deep focus, close your work, stretch your body, and allow your mind to wander gently. Take a short walk, breathe deeply, or simply sit in stillness for a few minutes. Nature, music, or a few moments of silence can do more to restore your concentration than hours of restless distraction.

Physical renewal also matters. The mind draws its strength from the vitality of the body. After long periods of thought, engage in simple movement — a walk, a stretch, or light exercise. Let your body balance the intensity of mental work with motion and breath. As your muscles awaken, your mind becomes clearer again.

Emotional renewal is equally essential. The mind cannot sustain focus when burdened by resentment, anxiety, or fatigue. Forgive quickly, release tension, and let go of self-criticism. These small acts of inner kindness free up immense mental energy. Remember that poise, courage, and focus all spring from inner balance.

Recovery also includes joy. Pleasure, laughter, conversation, art, or time spent with loved ones all serve to replenish the heart. Joy is not a distraction from your purpose; it is the fuel that keeps purpose alive. A mind that knows both intensity and lightness works with greater grace and endurance.

Think of focus and recovery as two halves of the same cycle, inhalation and exhalation, day and night, tide and retreat. You cannot have one without the other. When you balance them, you build sustainable concentration that does not burn out but grows stronger over time.

This rhythm of flow and renewal applies to every area of life. In work, it allows for deep productivity without fatigue. In learning, it turns study into discovery. In relationships, it allows presence without depletion. It is the rhythm of nature itself, of effort followed by rest, silence after sound, winter before spring.

To sustain peak focus, you must live in harmony with this rhythm. The person who works with awareness of balance, who knows when to engage and when to release, will go farther than the one who pushes blindly. Concentration is not a struggle to hold the mind still; it is the art of aligning yourself with the natural flow of energy, knowing when to channel it and when to let it replenish itself.

When you understand this balance, your focus becomes effortless and enduring. You begin to work not from tension but from strength, not from haste but from harmony. Each period of concentration becomes a joy, and each moment of rest, a renewal of your power.

ꙮ

15

LIVING BY YOUR IDEALS

Concentrating on Your Vision

Through our paltry stir and strife, glows the wished ideal.
And longing moulds in clay, what life carves in the marble real.

— *James Russell Lowell*

Every life is shaped by the ideals it holds. Whether you are conscious of it or not, your ideals, the visions of what you believe possible and desirable, guide your thoughts, decisions, and direction. They are the compass of your character and the blueprint of your destiny.

We often speak of idealists as if they are dreamers, detached from reality. Yet in truth, every person is an idealist to some degree. We all live by mental images of what we believe life could be. Every invention, every great work of art, every reform in society began first as an idea, an ideal, in someone's mind. Everything that now exists was once imagined.

When you control your thoughts, you become a creator. You receive ideas that align with your highest nature and give them shape through effort, patience, and will. Every time you focus your mind on an ideal, whether it be courage, kindness, excellence, or integrity, you are quietly moulding your character in its image. The ideal is the seed; concentration and effort are the soil and water that bring it to life.

You are responsible for every condition you go through, either consciously or unconsciously. The next step you take determines the one that follows. This simple truth places immense power in your hands. By choosing your ideals and holding them faithfully, you choose the direction of your life. By concentrating on each step as you go along, you save years of wasted wandering.

Concentrate upon your ideals until they take form in action. Through concentration, you convert vision into reality. Your future is not built by chance, but by the steady shaping of your ideals into habits.

The ideals you held in the past determine where you stand today. If you wish to create a brighter future, begin now to cultivate the ideals that will sustain it. Many people fail not for lack of ability, but because their ideals shift too easily. They change direction at every difficulty, never realising that perseverance is the bridge between imagination and achievement. When you abandon your ideals, you lose the very power that could have brought them to life.

Consider a simple example. You wake in the morning resolved to remain calm and patient throughout the day. This is your ideal of poise. Then an unexpected event or irritation arises, and before you know it, you have lost your temper. The ideal vanishes in the heat of emotion. But if, in that instant, you had remembered your ideal, had paused for even a second to recall the image of the calm, self-possessed person you aspire to be, you would have acted differently. You lose your poise when you forget your ideal.

Every lapse of attention weakens willpower. Every moment of recollection strengthens it. Holding to your ideals develops willpower as surely as exercise strengthens muscle. To live by your ideals is not to dream idly, but to act consciously, moment by moment, in alignment with what you most respect and admire.

Why do so many people fail to achieve what they desire? Because they do not hold to their ideal until it becomes a mental habit. They begin with conviction but falter with distraction or discouragement. Success comes only when you sustain the vision until it becomes second nature. You must think your ideal, speak it, live it, and return to it whenever you stray. The mind must be trained to hold the image steadily until it shapes the world around it.

The statement "I am that which I think myself to be" is not a poetic exaggeration. It is a psychological truth. You become the sum of your habitual thoughts and intentions. Therefore, give your ideals time, hours of consistent, persistent thought. Reflect on them daily. Measure your actions by them.

No person climbs a mountain by wishing himself to the summit. He must climb, step by step, breath by breath, refusing to stop when the ascent grows difficult. Likewise, no one escapes the monotony or confusion of life by merely wishing for change. He must will the change and act on it with concentrated effort.

If you find yourself standing still or slipping backwards, do not blame fate or circumstance. The cause lies within, and so does the remedy. Do not pity yourself; examine yourself. Ask where your ideals have faltered. Are you still holding to them as firmly as before? Have you allowed discouragement, distraction, or self-doubt to weaken them? The moment you rediscover your ideals, you rediscover your strength.

Self-pity, resentment, and complaint are the thoughts of failure. They dissipate concentration and invite defeat. Replace them with self-responsibility and self-trust. You are your greatest ally and your most dependable source of progress.

Just as doctors renew their Hippocratic oath to remind themselves of their duty and purpose, each of us must renew our inner vows—our personal oaths of purpose and integrity. We must remind ourselves of the higher laws that govern our lives. When you do not know what to think or say, use these words:

Let the troubles and responsibilities of life come thick and fast. I am ready for them. My soul is unconquerable. I represent the Infinite Law of force, or all power. This God within is my all-sufficient strength and ever-present help in times of trouble. The more the difficulties, the greater its triumphs through me. The harder my trials, the faster I grow in the development of my inherent strength. Let all else fail me. This interior reliance is all-sufficient. The right must prevail. I demand wisdom and power to know and follow the right. My higher self is all-wise. I now draw nearer to it.

Living by your ideals gives your life unity, direction, and moral power. It prevents drift and brings harmony to your actions. Your ideals lift you above circumstance, for when your mind holds firmly to what is noble and enduring, external conditions lose their sway.

A person without ideals lives at the mercy of events. A person with ideals shapes events. Your ideals define not only what you strive for, but also who you become in the process. Concentrate on them with patience and conviction until they become the unshakable centre of your being.

ཐུ

16

CONCENTRATION AND PROFESSIONAL SUCCESS

Concentrating on Your Work and Purpose

In the modern workplace, the greatest challenge is not lack of talent but lack of focus. Offices, once designed for work, have become arenas of noise, movement, and constant interruption. Open desks, phones that never stop buzzing, endless notifications, and meetings without purpose scatter attention into fragments. Even the most capable mind loses its depth in such a storm. Concentration has become a rare skill, yet it remains the foundation of all professional success.

A person can only think one thought at a time, but the modern world demands many. We switch from emails to calls, from one tab to another, pretending to multitask, while our attention thins like worn cloth. Each interruption costs more than a few seconds. Research shows it takes several minutes to regain full focus after a single distraction. The price of divided attention is hidden but enormous, as it turns meaningful work into perpetual catching up.

Consider the typical office morning. You sit down with the intent to finish a report. Before opening the document, you glance at your phone. Two messages, one irrelevant, one irritating. You reply quickly, only to notice a new email. Halfway through reading it, a colleague asks, "Got a minute?" Twenty minutes later, you return to your report, but your mind feels restless. What should have taken an hour now takes three. The body stayed at the desk, but the mind wandered the whole time.

This is how most professionals live: constantly present, rarely focused. They confuse activity with accomplishment. The difference is vast. Activity is motion without meaning; accomplishment is motion guided by concentration. The one who learns to bring the mind wholly into the task will always rise above those who scatter theirs among distractions.

To cultivate this strength, begin by understanding your workspace. Every environment contains both tools for concentration and traps for distraction. A cluttered desk scatters thoughts. Excessive noise pulls your mind outward. Unnecessary conversations drain energy. Even digital clutter—dozens of open windows, constant alerts, multitasking software—creates a mental fog. Bring order to your space, and you will begin to bring order to your mind.

Create small rituals that prepare you for deep work. Before beginning, clear your desk of everything unrelated to the task. Close all browser tabs except the one you need. Put your phone out of sight. If you work in an open office, use headphones or soft music to define a mental boundary. These small acts signal to your brain that it is time to focus. Consistency in ritual builds consistency in attention.

In many workplaces, the loudest voice is mistaken for the most productive. Meetings stretch on without decisions, and interruptions are treated as collaboration. But concentration does not grow in noise. It grows in respect over time. Professionals who value their focus learn to protect it firmly but courteously. They say, "Can we talk at 3 p.m. instead?" instead of allowing every request to break their rhythm. Those who treat their attention as precious eventually become the ones others rely on for clarity.

Distraction also arises from emotional unrest. Office politics, competition, and the constant comparison of progress can quietly consume thought. You may find yourself replaying a comment from a superior or worrying about another's success. This is an internal distraction, often more damaging than external noise. Concentration demands emotional discipline. Let go of resentment and envy. The mind that clings to them cannot think clearly. Focus instead on what you control, your effort, your conduct, your improvement.

Technology, which promises productivity, often undermines it. The very tools meant to help, like email, messaging apps, project trackers, become instruments of fragmentation when used without restraint. Professionals who check notifications every few minutes live in a state of partial attention, unable to enter the deeper rhythm where creativity happens. The solution is not withdrawal, but structure. Check messages at set intervals. Turn off alerts during work blocks. Batch similar tasks together so your mind stays within one mode. Guard your deep work hours as fiercely as appointments with your most important client.

If your work involves long hours or creative problem-solving, you will need periods of uninterrupted solitude. Deep concentration thrives in silence. Great discoveries, great designs, and great writing have never come from multitasking, but have come from immersion. Make time each day, even for an hour, to enter this state. Begin by focusing on one small, well-defined problem. Resist the urge to jump to another until it is complete. The mind, once trained to stay with one thought, begins to find satisfaction in completion itself.

Fatigue is another silent thief of concentration. Long hours, skipped meals, and constant stress erode patience and focus. A tired mind wanders easily. Learn to work in cycles: focus deeply, then rest deliberately. A short walk, a few deep breaths, or a moment away from the screen can reset attention. Rest is not laziness; it is maintenance. The professionals who sustain excellence over decades are those who understand the rhythm of effort and renewal.

There will also be days when concentration feels impossible. When noise, stress, or emotion seems stronger than willpower. On such days, reduce your ambition to something achievable. Do one task completely. Finish one call with total presence. Even a single act done well restores confidence and calms the mind. The discipline of focus is not built in grand moments but in these small victories, repeated until they become habit.

In the workplace, there is a quiet distinction between those who are merely busy and those who are deeply effective. The busy person is constantly reacting to messages, to people, to problems. The effective one acts from intention. Concentration gives you that choice. It allows you to pause before replying, to think before speaking, to see before judging. Over time, this clarity earns trust. Others may rush, but they will turn to you when it matters most, because your focus brings results.

True professional success is not measured by how much you do, but by how much of yourself you bring to what you do. The most successful workers are not superhuman; they are simply fully present. Their attention does not wander when they listen, plan, or create. They have learned that to give full concentration to the workspace is to give respect to the task, to the team, and to oneself.

You can begin today. Choose one hour and make it sacred to concentration. During that time, no messages, no noise, no multitasking. Only one task and one intention. Observe how deeply you can work when the mind stops scattering itself. At first, it will be difficult, but soon that hour will become the most productive and peaceful part of your day. Expand it slowly, and you will discover that focus is not only a professional skill, but also a state of mind that transforms all work into purpose.

Concentration restores dignity to labour. It turns the ordinary office desk into a place of mastery. It brings depth where there was distraction and meaning where there was routine. The concentrated worker is rare, but indispensable. Wherever such a person is found, order follows, progress begins, and success endures.

To give full concentration to your work is not to isolate yourself from life—it is to enter life more completely. For when the mind is wholly engaged, work ceases to be struggle and becomes creation. That is the quiet secret behind every lasting success.

ꟾ

17

DEEP LEARNING

Concentrating on the Art of Study

Education is not the simple gathering of information; it is the shaping of the mind. True learning does not come from how much one studies, but from how deeply one attends. A distracted student may read for hours and remember little. A concentrated one may study for a short time and grasp the essence of a subject completely. Concentration is the difference between memorising facts and understanding truth.

The modern world makes concentration in study more difficult than ever before. Students live surrounded by noise, in digital noise, social noise, and mental noise. Phones vibrate, notifications flash, and messages arrive in a constant rhythm. Each one promises a moment of interest and steals a minute of thought. The mind that should dive deep keeps skimming the surface. A student who studies with the phone beside them studies with a divided mind. Even when the screen lies silent, the anticipation of distraction is enough to break the thread of thought.

A classroom or study room should be a place of attention, yet it often becomes a place of performance. Students worry about grades, comparisons, or appearances more than about comprehension. True concentration is quiet and humble. It does not seek to impress; it seeks to understand. To study with focus is to forget oneself—to be absorbed completely in the problem before you, as if no one else exists.

Many students confuse time spent with effort given. They measure progress by hours instead of by depth. A mind that drifts for five hours learns less than a mind that is present for one. The secret of effective study is not longer sessions, but fuller ones. Every subject requires periods of total absorption, when the mind wrestles with ideas until they become its own. This can happen only when distractions are shut out completely.

The first step toward focused study is preparation. Before you begin, set your space in order. Clear your desk of everything unrelated to the subject. Keep your phone in another room. Open only the books and notes you need. Each small act of preparation tells your brain: "This matters." The environment becomes an ally in concentration. A cluttered space invites distraction; a clean one invites focus.

Next, set a clear goal for your session. Instead of saying, "I will study history," say, "I will understand the causes of the French Revolution." The mind needs direction to stay anchored. A vague plan allows it to wander; a specific one keeps it sharp. Work in cycles. Forty minutes of deep focus followed by a short break. During those minutes, resist every impulse to drift. When you feel the urge to check something trivial, remind yourself that curiosity can wait. The world will still be there when you finish.

Students often complain that they cannot focus because the subject is dull. Yet dullness is not in the subject; it is in the state of attention. A concentrated mind can find interest even in the simplest material, for it begins to see patterns and meanings others miss. Boredom is the sign of a restless mind, not a poor topic. Once the mind learns to stay with one thing, that thing becomes alive.

Teachers, too, play a role in cultivating concentration. A teacher who merely delivers information cannot hold attention for long. But one who awakens curiosity, who connects the lesson to life, helps students focus naturally. When learning feels meaningful, attention follows without force. The most powerful classrooms are not those filled with silence, but those filled with engagement, where every student's mind is awake, not merely present.

Distraction is not only external; it often comes from within. Anxiety about exams, fear of failure, or comparison with others can cloud focus. Worry divides the mind between the task and imagined outcomes. When you study, study only. Do not think of results. Let learning be its own purpose. The more you give your whole attention to understanding, the better the results will follow. Concentration is not achieved through pressure, but through interest and presence.

Another obstacle to focus is fatigue. Late-night study sessions filled with caffeine and exhaustion create only the illusion of effort. The tired mind reads words but fails to absorb meaning. Rest is part of the study. A well-rested mind grasps in an hour what a weary one cannot hold in three. Balance is not laziness; it is strategy. Sleep, movement, and fresh air are tools of concentration as vital as books and notes.

Technology, when used wisely, can support focus instead of harming it. Digital tools that block notifications, time your sessions, or limit distractions can serve as modern companions to discipline. Yet no tool can replace self-control. The power to say, "Not now" to every temptation is the foundation of concentration. Students who develop this power early carry it into every part of life.

Study with intention, not habit. Before beginning, remind yourself why the subject matters. Every field of knowledge connects to something greater, the science to curiosity, literature to empathy, history to perspective. When the mind remembers purpose, attention strengthens. When purpose is forgotten, study becomes mechanical and lifeless.

Concentration also grows through repetition. Each time you bring your wandering mind back to the page, you strengthen it. Do not be discouraged when focus slips; bring it back gently. Over time, the mind learns to obey. The student who perseveres through distraction gains not only knowledge but mastery over their own thoughts. That mastery is the true goal of education.

To give full concentration to learning is to respect your own potential. It is to say, "I am capable of depth." Each focused study session builds patience, memory, and discipline—qualities that outlast any exam. Education is not about passing tests; it is about training the mind to think, observe, and understand. Concentration is both the method and the reward of that training.

Imagine two students in the same library. One sits surrounded by notes, checking messages every few minutes, sighing in frustration. The other sits with a single notebook, lost in study, time forgotten. When the day ends, the first has gathered fragments; the second has gained insight. Both worked hard, but only one worked wholly. Concentration made the difference.

If you wish to excel, learn to enjoy the act of focus itself. Find satisfaction in small moments of clarity, the sentence understood, the concept mastered, the problem solved. These moments are proof that your mind is awakening to its power. Once you taste that strength, distraction begins to lose its charm.

Learning with concentration is not only an academic skill; it is preparation for life. The ability to think deeply, to stay with a problem until it yields, will serve you in every career and relationship that follows. The student who learns to command their attention early will always move through life with confidence and composure.

Education is not the memorisation of lessons but the concentration of the mind upon truth. Those who learn to focus in youth carry that gift forever. Let your study not be a race against time, but a journey into understanding. The more deeply you can think, the more freely you can live. Concentration is not just the secret of education—it is the essence of wisdom.

ℵ

18

CONCENTRATION IN RELATIONSHIPS

Presence and Attention to Others

The power of concentration does not apply only to personal goals or professional pursuits. It also governs the quality of our relationships—how deeply we connect, how well we understand others, and how harmoniously we live together. To truly relate to another person, you must be present. Presence is the highest form of attention, and attention is love made visible. When your mind is scattered, you do not truly hear, see, or feel what the other person is communicating. You may nod, reply, or even sympathise outwardly, but inwardly, you are divided. Your thoughts wander to your own concerns, and you miss the living moment unfolding before you.

Concentration is what bridges that gap. When you give someone your full, quiet attention, you affirm their worth. You recognise their humanity. In that instant, you step beyond self-interest and become fully available to the shared experience. This act of mindful attention has the power to heal misunderstandings, deepen bonds, and create a space of mutual respect.

Most relationships suffer not because of a lack of care, but because of a lack of focused awareness. We are too often preoccupied with what we want to say next, how we appear, or how we might respond. We listen to reply, not to understand. Concentration restores the ability to listen wholly. It teaches us to suspend judgment, to quiet the inner chatter, and to let another person's words, tone, and emotions fully register before we act.

There is tremendous creative power in stillness. When you are quiet inside, you can sense what another person truly means, beyond their words. This kind of listening requires humility and strength. You no longer insist that your opinion prevail. You do not rush to fill the silence. You listen not only with your ears but with your mind and heart. This deeper attention allows empathy to arise naturally. You begin to feel what the other feels, without losing yourself in their emotion.

Concentration in relationships is not only about listening, but also about being mindful of what you communicate. Your words, your tone, your manner of speaking, all reveal your inner state. If your thoughts are hurried or clouded by agitation, it will show. But if you speak from a mind that is calm and focused, your words carry clarity and weight. People feel the difference instantly. Concentration refines communication because it aligns thought and expression.

In moments of disagreement, concentration becomes an anchor. When conflict arises, the untrained mind reacts instinctively, like raising its voice, defending, accusing, or withdrawing. The concentrated mind pauses before responding. It creates a space in which emotion can settle and understanding can grow. Instead of reacting from anger or fear, you act from composure and principle. This ability to hold your poise when others lose theirs is one of the highest demonstrations of self-mastery.

True concentration also involves discernment, knowing when to speak and when to remain silent. Silence is not withdrawal; it is often the most powerful form of presence. It allows the other person's thoughts to surface and your own insights to form. Many great friendships and partnerships thrive on this kind of silence, a shared stillness that communicates understanding beyond words.

Relationships are mirrors. They reflect not only who others are, but who we are. When you meet irritation, impatience, or jealousy in others, use it as a prompt to examine yourself. Where does this reaction arise within me? Why am I unsettled? Concentration in relationships begins with self-awareness, for we cannot give to others what we have not yet cultivated within. A calm mind radiates calmness. A focused heart invites focus in return.

Concentration also teaches patience. Every person moves at their own rhythm of thought and feeling. When you are truly attentive, you begin to sense this rhythm. You no longer force others to conform to your pace. You give them the time and space to express themselves. This patient's attention often dissolves resistance and invites honesty.

In love, friendship, family, or work, relationships flourish when both people are fully present. Presence creates safety, and safety allows truth to emerge. When you are concentrated in your interactions, you make the other person feel seen, heard, and valued. This, more than eloquence or advice, is what strengthens human bonds.

To practice concentration in relationships, begin simply. When you are with someone, be with them completely. Set aside your phone, your distractions, your preoccupations. Look at them when they speak. Listen as though nothing else exists for that moment. Notice their tone, expression, and the emotion behind their words. If your mind drifts, gently bring it back. When you speak, do so with intention and clarity. Let your words rise from understanding, not impulse.

Gradually, this practice transforms your relationships. Conversations become richer, misunderstandings rarer, and affection deeper. You begin to experience connection not as effort, but as natural harmony. The same inner stillness that helps you focus on work now helps you see the people around you with compassion and depth.

Concentration brings harmony to the outer world by first establishing harmony within. When your thoughts are centred, you are not easily swayed by others' moods or opinions. You bring stability to every interaction. You become a quiet force of understanding, a presence others trust and gravitate toward.

ꟸ

19

CONCENTRATING AMID CONSTANT CONNECTION

We live in an age of unprecedented connection and unprecedented distraction. The same devices that put the world's knowledge at our fingertips also scatter our thoughts. Every sound, message, and screen invites our attention elsewhere. In this constant flood of information, concentration has become both rare and revolutionary. To think deeply today is to rebel against noise.

Our minds are not built for endless stimulation. They are built for rhythm, periods of focus and rest, attention and reflection. Yet digital life offers no such rhythm. It pulls us from one novelty to another, training the brain to expect interruption. Each click brings a small surge of excitement, and the mind begins to crave it. What was once curiosity becomes compulsion. The result is a restless mind that cannot stay still long enough to understand, create, or even rest.

Consider the ordinary digital morning. Before getting out of bed, the first reflex is to check the phone. Messages, news, and notifications rush in. Within minutes, your attention has been divided among dozens of small concerns. By the time you begin your actual work, your focus is already scattered. You have been awake for only an hour, yet you have given away your best attention to things that did not matter.

The digital age rewards speed, not depth. We scroll through headlines, skim through emails, and jump between tasks. We feel busy, even productive, but rarely fulfilled. Shallow attention gives the illusion of knowledge without the stability of understanding. The tragedy is not that we lack information, but that we no longer stay with it long enough to turn it into wisdom.

Concentration in this era begins with awareness. Notice how often you reach for your phone when bored, anxious, or uncertain. Each time you do, you are teaching your mind that silence must be filled and stillness avoided. Yet all true thinking arises from stillness. Creativity, insight, and clarity come not when the mind is overstimulated, but when it is calm enough to see connections that noise obscures.

To reclaim your attention, you must begin to control your environment. Technology is not the enemy; the absence of discipline is. Decide when and how you will engage with the digital world. Do not let it decide for you. Set boundaries: no screens during meals, no notifications during deep work, no scrolling before sleep. Protect the first and last hour of your day from screens entirely. These small separations create space for reflection and restore rhythm to the mind.

One of the greatest thieves of modern concentration is multitasking. We imagine we are doing many things at once, but in truth, we are only switching rapidly between them. Each switch fragment thought and drains energy. The cost is invisible but immense: reduced creativity, slower progress, more errors, and chronic mental fatigue. Concentration demands the opposite approach—unitasking. Do one thing at a time and give it your full attention. When it is done, move to the next. This simple discipline is now a radical act.

Digital communication, too, requires conscious restraint. Emails, messages, and group chats can consume entire days without producing anything meaningful. Most are not urgent. Create windows in your schedule for communication, and close them outside those times. The mind cannot think deeply when it is always half-listening for a notification. The professional who checks messages once in the morning and once in the afternoon often accomplishes more than the one who checks them fifty times a day.

Social media, perhaps the most powerful attention trap of all, feeds on emotion. Its design is deliberate, it rewards reaction, not reflection. Every like, every outrage, every image competes for your mental energy. The more time you spend there, the more restless you become, and the harder it grows to focus on anything sustained or serious. To regain clarity, you must starve the habit. Remove apps from your phone, limit your exposure, and replace scrolling with reading. The mind that once sought instant updates will, in time, rediscover the deeper satisfaction of thought.

Concentration in the digital age also means learning to endure boredom again. Boredom is not a flaw in life; it is the doorway to imagination. When the mind is not constantly stimulated, it begins to wander inward, to think, reflect, and create. Many of the world's great ideas were born not in moments of activity but in moments of quiet. Allow yourself to be unreachable sometimes. Let your attention rest. The mind that is never still cannot grow.

If you work or study with digital tools, learn to use them with purpose. Before opening your computer, decide exactly what you intend to do. Write it down if necessary. Then do only that. Do not open new tabs out of habit. Do not check unrelated sites "for a minute.' Every small act of distraction weakens discipline. The strength of your concentration depends on the number of decisions you refuse to make while working.

A practical method is what some call the "digital fast." Choose a time, perhaps a few hours each week—when you deliberately disconnect from all screens. Spend that time in physical activity, reading, or reflection. At first, you may feel anxious or restless. That is withdrawal. The mind, accustomed to constant noise, struggles with silence. Stay with it. Gradually, a different kind of clarity appears—the kind that feels like breathing fresh air after a long time indoors.

Another form of practice is attention training. Each time you notice your mind wandering while online, pause. Ask yourself what you were seeking before you drifted. Bring your attention back to that purpose. These small returns build strength. The goal is not to fight distraction endlessly, but to regain the ability to choose where your attention goes. Freedom begins with that choice.

Digital life also erodes patience. We expect everything instantly, answers, messages, results. When progress feels slow, frustration arises. Concentration requires the opposite temperament: patience, endurance, and the willingness to think through difficulty. The ability to sit with a complex idea, to let it unfold without immediate reward, is now a form of power. The person who can do so will always outthink and outcreate those who cannot.

Parents and teachers must also understand this new landscape. Children are growing up with attention shaped by screens from infancy. If we wish to raise minds capable of depth, we must teach them how to focus before they learn how to swipe. Limit screen exposure, encourage reading, and create spaces for boredom and play. The earlier the habit of concentration begins, the stronger it becomes.

Ultimately, technology amplifies whatever habits already exist. A scattered mind becomes more scattered with devices; a disciplined mind becomes more powerful. The solution is not rejection but mastery. Use technology as a tool, not a master. Let it serve your goals rather than consume them.

The digital age has given us incredible access, but also a choice: to skim or to see, to react or to reflect, to consume or to create. Concentration determines which path we take. The person who can focus deeply in this distracted world holds a decisive advantage. They think longer, listen better, and produce work of greater meaning and beauty.

Concentration is not about withdrawing from the digital world, but about learning to live consciously within it. To pause before reacting. To choose before clicking. To read slowly where others scroll quickly. When you control your attention, you reclaim your mind, and in doing so, you rediscover your humanity.

In every era, progress has belonged to those who could think clearly. The tools may change, but the law remains the same: the power of thought depends on the power of concentration. In this age of constant connection, the deepest connection you can make is with your own mind. Protect it fiercely. Train it daily. Let it rest often. For in the stillness behind the screen lies the only kind of freedom that technology cannot give—the freedom to think.

ꕥ

20

NURTURING ATTENTION

Concentrating in the Early Years

Every child is born with the seed of attention. You can see it in the way an infant stares at a moving light, or how a toddler studies a leaf as if it holds the secret of the world. This natural focus is pure and instinctive. It comes not from effort, but from curiosity. Yet as children grow, this precious ability often begins to fade, not because they lose interest in the world, but because the world begins to lose interest in their pace.

Modern childhood is full of movement, noise, and stimulation. Television, games, and constant schedules fill every quiet moment. Even learning has become hurried. Many parents and teachers, anxious about performance, push children to absorb more information instead of helping them engage deeply with one thing at a time. The result is early fatigue of attention. Children begin to skim life the way adults skim screens, quickly, restlessly, without wonder.

Concentration in young minds cannot be forced; it must be nurtured. It grows best in calm and simplicity. A child cannot focus when surrounded by constant noise or corrected at every step. The ability to attend develops through patience and freedom, the freedom to explore, repeat, fail, and return. A young child absorbed in stacking blocks or drawing in silence is not wasting time. In those moments of complete absorption, the child is building the foundations of thought.

The greatest obstacle to concentration in children today is overstimulation. Every environment competes for its senses: bright screens, background television, quick-cut cartoons, and toys that flash and talk. These train the mind to expect constant novelty. The more stimulation a child receives, the less capable they become of staying with quiet things. Their attention begins to fragment before it has fully formed.

To cultivate concentration, children must be given the chance to slow down. Replace noise with space. Give them fewer toys but better ones, the things that invite imagination rather than command reaction. Wooden blocks, puzzles, art materials, and books are companions that grow with the child. Unlike digital toys, they demand active thought and reward patience. The child learns not only to focus, but to create.

The environment in which a child lives speaks silently to their mind. A tidy, peaceful room invites calm; a chaotic one invites restlessness. Even the presence of a parent absorbed in their own screen sends a message about what deserves attention. Children learn not from what we say, but from what we model. When adults move constantly between devices, children imitate that rhythm. When adults pause, listen, and attend, children follow suit.

It is easy to underestimate how much a child perceives. They notice tone more than words, presence more than instruction. When you listen to a child with full attention, without checking your phone or rushing to respond, you are teaching them what attention feels like. They begin to understand that focus is an act of respect. It is how we show care for people and for tasks.

Schools often face the same challenge. Large classes, rigid schedules, and excessive testing create pressure that fragments focus. True education requires time for reflection and repetition. Young minds need to linger on ideas until they become clear. Teachers who cultivate concentration give students the gift of ownership over their learning. When a child discovers that they can stay with a problem until it makes sense, they gain confidence that no grade can replace.

Play is also one of the most powerful teachers of concentration. A child at play is a child at work. In unstructured play, they learn to set their own goals, experiment, and persist. Interrupting this natural process too often weakens it. Allowing children to become deeply involved in play, even if it looks aimless, develops the same mental endurance that later becomes useful in study and work.

Parents often mistake movement for energy and noise for enthusiasm. Yet true focus in children often appears as stillness. When a child is quietly absorbed, it is not a sign of withdrawal but of engagement. They are building inner order. Every time they stay with a task longer than before, they are strengthening the muscle of attention. Applaud that effort more than speed or cleverness.

Discipline is another misunderstood concept in early learning. To demand silence or obedience without understanding does not build concentration, it builds fear. But to guide gently, to create a rhythm of work and rest, helps the child develop inner control. Establish regular times for study, play, and rest. Predictability creates security, and security allows attention to flourish.

The influence of technology must also be approached carefully. Screens can educate, but they can also overwhelm. For very young children, digital stimulation replaces imagination with imitation. For older ones, it becomes a habit that dulls curiosity. Limit screen exposure, not as punishment, but as protection. Encourage them to experience the real world through touch, movement, and conversation. A child who learns to find interest in nature, books, and human company will always have a strong attention span.

Another hidden barrier to focus in children is stress. When a child feels anxious, unsafe, or criticised, their attention collapses inward. Fear makes learning impossible. Compassion restores it. Encourage effort rather than perfection. Celebrate curiosity more than correct answers. When children feel secure, their minds naturally open. Concentration is not a demand we make—it is a response we earn.

The best gift you can give a child is not entertainment but engagement. Share activities that require patience and presence: gardening, cooking, reading aloud, or building something together. These experiences teach rhythm and repetition. They show that satisfaction comes not from speed, but from doing something with care.

Each stage of childhood offers opportunities to strengthen concentration. The infant who follows a moving object, the toddler who stacks blocks, the school-age child who reads for pleasure, all are practising the same essential skill. Support them by slowing down with them. When the world rushes, let your home be a place where attention can rest.

In time, a child raised with these habits develops a rare strength: the ability to think independently. They are not easily swayed by noise or novelty. They can listen, learn, and create with calm purpose. This is not only the foundation of learning; it is the foundation of character.

Every great thinker, artist, and leader once sat as a child, absorbed in something simple, a drawing, a puzzle, a question. In that stillness, the habit of focus was born. That habit, once formed, becomes the silent ally of a lifetime. If we wish to raise children capable of depth, we must protect their early attention from the chaos of speed.

Concentration is the first language of intelligence. It begins not in classrooms or books, but in the quiet of early wonder. When we teach children to stay with what they love, to watch, to listen, to finish what they start—we give them a gift that the noise of the world cannot take away. For in that simple act of staying with one thing until it reveals itself, a child learns not only how to think, but how to live

ꕥ

21

THE BALANCED MIND

Concentration is one of the highest human abilities, but like all powers, it must be used with wisdom and moderation. To live fully, you must know not only how to focus but also how to release that focus. Many people learn to work with great intensity but never learn how to rest their minds. They drive themselves constantly, carrying their business, their worries, and their ambitions everywhere they go.

Do not make the mistake of taking your work home in your thoughts. To be successful, you must indeed learn to concentrate, but do not become a slave to your concentration. The mind, like the body, has limits. If you burn both ends of the candle, the flame of vitality will soon go out.

Some people sit in a church or temple but do not hear the sermon because their minds are still on their business. They attend the theatre or a family gathering yet find no joy in it, for their thoughts never leave their work. Even when they go to bed, they toss and turn, their minds filled with unfinished tasks and imaginary problems. They wonder why sleep eludes them, unaware that they are victims of ungoverned concentration.

This kind of attention is not true concentration; it is compulsion. It is involuntary, obsessive, and unhealthy. It drains the mind's energy instead of refining it. Any thought that rules you instead of being ruled by you becomes destructive. You must remember this truth: he who does not rule his own mind is not truly successful, no matter what he achieves outwardly.

The balanced mind is the mind that knows when to focus and when to let go. It is steady but flexible, alert yet calm. It works when work is required and rests when rest is needed. It can give itself completely to one task, and then turn away from it without strain or regret. This is not indifference; it is mastery.

When your mind becomes one-pointed during work, it should become equally restful during leisure. True concentration is not about tightening the mind; it is about directing it at will. You should be able to pick up a subject, hold it, and then lay it down, just as easily as you would lift and set aside a tool.

To maintain balance, you must learn to deliberately shift your attention. This practice is as vital as learning to focus. When you finish your work for the day, consciously close that mental chapter. Perform a small ritual that signals the end of work, like organise your desk, take a short walk, or sit quietly for a moment and affirm to yourself, "My work for today is done. My mind is free." By doing so, you teach your subconscious to release tension and prepare for restoration.

Balanced concentration also involves giving the mind a wholesome variety. Engage in activities that refresh it, such as reading something uplifting, enjoying music, being in nature, or spending time with loved ones without distraction. These are not idle pastimes; they are essential counterweights to intense focus. A rested mind returns to its work sharper, more creative, and more capable of insight.

Self-control lies at the heart of balance. You should be able to hold your thoughts on a subject as long as needed, but also to withdraw them at will. When you cannot stop thinking about something, when a problem or worry haunts you day and night, you are no longer its master; you are its prisoner. True concentration gives freedom, not bondage.

Learn to listen to your body's quiet messages. When fatigue, irritability, or restlessness set in, they are signals that the mind needs rest or a change of activity. The wise do not ignore these signals. They know that forcing the mind beyond its natural rhythm leads to exhaustion and diminishing returns.

Balance also means maintaining perspective. Your work, ambitions, and goals are important, but they are only parts of a larger whole. Life is not meant to be lived in fragments. Concentration, when rightly used, enhances every area of life rather than eclipsing it. It sharpens perception, deepens enjoyment, and enriches relationships, when balanced by rest, reflection, and appreciation.

A balanced mind is a creative mind. It is open to inspiration because it is not constantly strained. It is responsive to beauty and goodness because it is not dulled by fatigue or obsession. In its calmness lies its greatest power. From such a mind arise wisdom, patience, and peace.

To achieve this state, practice alternating between periods of intense focus and complete release. During work, be wholly absorbed. During rest, be wholly detached. If you work, work. If you play, play. If you rest, rest. Do each thing with your full attention, but never carry one state into another.

In this way, you will find not only greater efficiency but also greater happiness. The world will no longer seem rushed and overwhelming. You will move through it with quiet purpose, knowing that the same mind which can build, analyse, and solve can also feel, love, and enjoy.

Balance is not inaction; it is harmony. It is the art of aligning effort and rest, action and stillness, work and contemplation. The balanced mind neither races ahead nor lags. It moves with the rhythm of life itself.

ജ്ര

ꕥ

CONCLUSION

Living a Concentrated Life

You have come to the end of a journey that leads not outward, but inward. The greatest discoveries are not found in the world around you, but in the depths of your own awareness. Every page, every reflection, every exercise has been leading you to this realisation: the power to shape your life lies entirely within your mind.

Most people drift through their days without direction. They chase happiness, peace, and success as if these things existed somewhere far away. But they do not. They live within the reach of your thought. The more you learn to focus that thought, the more life begins to unfold according to your will. Concentration is not a harsh discipline; it is a return to your natural state of presence. It brings you back to yourself.

When you learn to concentrate, you stop scattering your strength. You no longer waste your energy on trivial distractions or anxious repetition. You begin to live from a deeper centre of calm awareness. You see more clearly, act more deliberately, and think with purpose. What once felt complicated begins to feel simple again. The noise fades. You discover that your attention, when directed with care and conviction, is creative power in its purest form.

The art of concentration is the art of living fully. It allows you to pour your whole being into what is before you, into your work, your relationships, your moments of rest. When your attention and your actions move in the same direction, life gathers meaning and force. You feel less divided. You begin to experience a quiet strength that does not rely on circumstances. This strength becomes your constant companion, your source of clarity in a noisy world.

But true concentration also teaches balance. There is a time to act with intensity and a time to let go completely. A focused mind that also knows how to rest becomes a steady flame that never burns out. Such a mind works with precision and lives with peace. When you learn to shift your attention consciously, to give your full self to each moment and then release it, you begin to experience freedom.

Every day offers you a new chance to practice this. You can learn to bring your mind back to your purpose whenever it wanders, to steady it when it trembles, to lift it when it grows weary. This daily practice is the quiet forge of transformation. Through it, will becomes habit, and habit becomes character. You begin to see results, not as sudden miracles, but as the steady unfolding of your own disciplined effort.

Life will always contain struggle, uncertainty, and change. You cannot control these entirely, but you can control how you meet them. The concentrated mind does not run from challenge; it faces it with composure. It listens, learns, and responds without fear. Each obstacle becomes an opportunity to grow stronger, more patient, and more self-aware.

As you move forward, let this be your understanding: concentration is not only a method for success, but a way of being. It is the practice of living awake. It means taking responsibility for where your mind goes, for what you feed it, and for how you use it. It is known that attention is the most powerful currency you have, and that whatever you give it to will grow.

Look within yourself and recognise the immense potential already there. You carry in your mind all the energy, intelligence, and imagination you need to build a meaningful life. Every great discovery, every work of art, every enduring achievement began as a thought held firmly until it took form. Your own life can be shaped in the same way.

So begin again, here, at the end. Decide what you wish to create, and give it your full attention. Guard your focus as you would your time, your energy, and your peace. Let your thoughts align with your ideals, and your actions will follow naturally.

Do this consistently, patiently, and with faith in your own ability, and life will open before you in ways you cannot yet imagine. You will find yourself calmer, stronger, and more alive than ever before. You will understand that mastery is not a destination, but a daily practice, a way of meeting the world with steady eyes and a quiet mind.

The power is already within you. It has always been there, waiting for your command. Choose to awaken it. Choose to direct it with purpose and integrity.

To live a concentrated life is to live freely and deeply. It is to meet each moment with presence, to act with strength, and to rest with peace. It is to discover, finally, that everything you seek has been within your grasp all along.

Now go inward, and begin.

ꟹ